T0328540

AGAINST THE GRAIN

AGAINST THE GRAIN

Six Men Who Shaped America

ROBERT UNDERHILL

Algora Publishing
New York

Library of Congress Cataloging-in-Publication Data —

Underhill, Robert, 1920-
   Against the grain: six men who shaped America / Robert Underhill.
      pages cm
   Includes bibliographical references and index.
      ISBN 978-1-62894-063-3 (soft cover: alk. paper) — ISBN 978-1-62894-064-0 (hard
cover: alk. paper) — ISBN 978-1-62894-065-7 (ebook) 1. Politicians—United States—
Attitudes. 2. Politicians—United States—Biography. 3. United States—Politics and
government—Moral and ethical aspects. I. Title.
   E176.U43 2014
   324.2092—dc23
   [B]

                              2013049448

Printed in the United States

For Sue—Beloved Daughter, Critic, and Inspiration.

TABLE OF CONTENTS

ACKNOWLEDGMENTS

One of the most quotable authors of the twentieth century, Winston Churchill, philosophized about writing a book. "Writing," said the venerable Britisher, "is an adventure. To begin with, it is a toy and amusement. Then it becomes a mistress; then a master, and next it becomes a tyrant. The last phase is that just as you are about to be reconciled to your servitude, you kill the monster and fling him to the public."

Although the author of this present book is the sole person to stand in the dock awaiting a verdict, there have been others who encouraged and abetted in the deed's perpetration.

An English philosopher and writer, Thomas Carlyle, wrote the line, "The history of the world is but the study of innumerable biographies."

In studies of and history and literature, my preference has tilted toward biography, i.e., to examine the careers, achievements, and motivations of men and women who have left us lasting effects. I believe that human beings, one man or one woman at a time, frequently have had effects in slowing or hastening the forces that make history. Often they were genuine prophets ahead of their time.

I am indebted to many persons for helping me pursue my mission. Inspiring teachers at Manchester University awakened my mind, and faculty colleagues there as well as later ones at Northwestern University and Iowa State University refused to let it stagnate. Particular faculty members were Ernest Wrage at Northwestern, Clarence Matterson at Iowa State, and Keith Huntress, the most literate man I've ever known, also from the latter institution.

I'd be remiss if I failed to mention appreciation to several generations of undergraduate and graduate students who enlivened my classes with friendly challenges that put a damper on pedant aloofness.

Although I use a computer as do other writers, I'm often at a loss with it, and without my guru, Professor Herb Harmison, this manuscript could never have been finished. In addition to Herb, I owe thanks to book clubs friend Dr. Chuck Jons and his wife Caroline, Pat Severson, Colleen Nutty, Mary Watkins, and Roy and Carol Zingg. These comrades as well as my long-time close friends Fred and Terry Schlunz listened to my ranting and ideas before they ever got onto paper. My bridge partner and dining companion, Margaret Maitland, has been patient enough to do likewise.

A book's production demands cooperation from many persons, and I am particularly indebted to our professional and ever courteous publishers—editors and other staff members—at Algora Publishing in New York.

Careful readers will note that I've drawn from books listed in the Bibliography as well as from magazines, journals, and newspapers. Archivists at the William R. Parks and Ellen Parks Library at Iowa State University, the Ames Public Library, and the National Archives in Washington, D.C. have been quick and accurate in honoring every request.

My greatest debt is to my daughter Sue and her husband Dr. Kenneth Mills. Sue offered ideas on organization and was constantly on the lookout for supporting materials for any one of my six principals. Ken was of immeasurable help when I got into difficulties of formatting and end notes.

There are shortcomings in every book, and whatever ones a scrutinizing reader may find in this book are faults of the author alone, who seeks your forgiveness.

Robert Underhill

PREFACE

In history books we read tales of men and women who spoke for ideas well in advance of their acceptance by the public; sometimes such heresy exacted heavy tolls — sacrifice of reputation, abandonment of personal goals, and loss of office or fortune. John Adams incurred the wrath of neighbors and risked the life of his pregnant wife Abigail as well as his own career when in 1770 he chose to defend in court British soldiers who had fired upon American revolutionaries in Boston. Abraham Lincoln would not yield to popular sentiment while speaking against slavery in southern Illinois during those epochal debates of 1858, nor would his opponent Stephen Douglas endorse the proviso for admitting Kansas as the fifteenth slave state under the Lecompton agreement even though he knew his heresy would most likely destroy his chances for the presidency. In another critical era, Eugene Debs was sent to a federal prison for defending freedom of speech amid the hysteria of World War I. Other individuals may be less known, but in speaking their consciences they left indelible marks on the pages of history.

Walter Lippmann, premier journalist of the mid-twentieth century, once wrote, "The final test of a leader is that he leaves behind him in other men the conviction and will to carry on." It follows, therefore, that a true leader must not always voice opinions dominant at his time, but, borrowing a metaphor from Daniel Webster, "must push his own skiff to shore."

Courage has many faces, and it appears in records of nearly every human society. Who can deny the courage of those pilgrims who put belongings and hope into a tiny vessel named the Mayflower and dared venture out into a vast and violent ocean? And then came pioneers armed only with grim determination who trekked into lands rife with perils of weather and fierce human defenders of traditional hunting grounds. Soldiers wearing Union blue or Confederate gray fell at Antietam, Chancellorsville, or Gettysburg in displays of dedication and courage. Likewise in two world wars, human individuals from differing nations sacrificed their lives for the causes they believed in.

Courage is useful to citizens and soldiers in times of war — a virtue which moves humans in uniform or civilian dress — to perform noble deeds. Surely, it is no disrespect to assert that sometimes physical courage may be more easily brought to bear when flags are flying and comrades are alongside than when one stands alone with only his or her conscience as a guide — few to cheer but many to hiss. Such is the plight of the rebel who severs party connections and alienates friends as he voices his moral convictions. The six persons profiled in this book were members of differing political parties, and each of them put aside personal goals by advocating measures unpopular at the time with most of the public.

Ignatius Donnelly was never a party regular; at one time he was a Democrat; later he became a Republican, and finally was the prime mover in formation of the People's Party. In his lifetime, he argued for redistribution of America's wealth and political control while the "White Man's Burden" and "Imperialism" were dominant credos of the country.

Mark Twain in referring to Theodore Roosevelt declared, "The President is clearly insane . . . and insanest upon war and its supreme glories." Echoing similar judgment Mark Hanna, Chairman of the Republican Party in the 1890s, asserted that Theodore Roosevelt should not be a vice-presidential candidate because he was a "madman" who would be only a heartbeat from the presidency. Roosevelt was a renegade, "a traitor to his caste," — a man born to the purple who castigated the "malefactors of great wealth" when he "should have been on the side of capital."

Eugene V. Debs was once a Republican and then a Democrat before becoming a Socialist. A five-time presidential candidate, he was imprisoned twice for speaking fearlessly for the American principle of free speech along with the rights of labor and the oppressed.

Robert La Follette, a nominal Republican, was a spokesman who gave voice to ideas contrary to that party's official pronouncements. He wanted to restrain the rampant practices of railroads and corporation magnates — and his attempts to do so set patterns that later federal administrators would follow.

George Norris was a long-time Republican before announcing himself an Independent. As a U.S. senator, he broke with dominant conservatives in his party and led the fight for more government built-and-controlled power facilities: federal dams, reforestation, electrification, and related endeavors, knowing that he would be confronted by hostility from friends, colleagues, and party Brahmins.

Henry A. Wallace was an American paradox whose scientific endeavors as a scientist tripled agricultural production, but politically he was a maverick who preached the gospel of reducing production in order to rescue embattled farmers and other wage-earners.

Ignatius Donnelly, Theodore Roosevelt, Robert La Follette, and George Norris were nominal Republicans as was Henry Wallace for a long time, even though he is best remembered for his service under Democratic administrations. At one time or another, Eugene Debs was identified with each of three parties: Republican, Democrat, or Socialist, but it was moral principles, not party affiliations, that guided his life.

What trait did these crusaders share? Every one of them had a high sense of moral obligation and in crises acted from that motivation rather than from social, family, or party allegiances — each willing to be outcast from usual supporters.

Donnelly, Theodore Roosevelt, Debs, La Follette, Norris, and Wallace are but six men selected from those who have had enough courage to go against the grain.

CHAPTER 1. IGNATIUS DONNELLY: APOSTLE OF PROTEST

"The whole idea is preposterous. Some crackpot is always coming up with a crazy theory of one sort or another." Other critics said the author must have been drunk or smoking Minnesota tobacco — a reference to marijuana, abundant in that state and in Iowa below it.

The crackpot was Ignatius Donnelly, and the time was 1882. Donnelly, a liberal Republican from Minnesota, had just published his first book, and in it he alleged,

> There once existed in the Atlantic Ocean, opposite the Mediterranean Sea, a large island, which was the remnant of an Atlantic continent, and known to the ancients as Atlantis... The description of this island given by Plato is not, as has been long supposed, fable, but verifiable history.[1]

The book, a product of Donnelly's fervent mind and limitless energy, was no novel but a serious attempt to demonstrate what he maintained was a historical truth.

Ignatius Donnelly was born in Philadelphia in 1831 and as a young man studied law, which to him was dull and unexciting; he preferred to read history or to write poetry. He knew that his father Philip Donnelly had abandoned Roman Catholicism, and perhaps that awareness may help explain the son's avoidance of using his own Catholic middle name, *Loyola*. Moreover, when Ignatius Donnelly entered his teen years, the city of Philadelphia was torn by a series of riots between Catholics and non-Catholics. Before order could be restored, twenty-four persons were dead, two Catholic churches had been burned, and extensive damage had been done to other Catholic properties.

The uproar left indelible scars on the young lad with his Irish heritage, and a quarter of a century later Donnelly would tell a Fourth of July audience:

> I can recollect that in my boyhood Philadelphia was afflicted with many riots; riots between whites and blacks, between natives and foreigners, between the different churches and different fire companies. All that has passed away. The public schools have cured it all. They have humanized the new generation.[2]

Donnelly was wrong in asserting that by the time he was an adolescent public schools had erased all friction among society's competing groups. On the contrary, it was a period when the United States saw the rise of one of its most shameful sects.

The "Native American", later called the "Know-Nothing" Party, sprouted when Donnelly was twenty-two years old. Concerned by the steadily growing number of immigrants, adherents to the new Party aimed to exclude any person not native born from holding federal, state, or municipal offices

The sect also urged the repeal of existing naturalization laws. "Know-Nothing" became the group's official name because its followers' response to any question regarding policy was, "I don't know." The dishonest answer was agreed upon because party members were sworn to secrecy.

Donnelly married at the age of twenty-five and with his bride left the City of Brotherly Love to set out for Minnesota, a land then considered by Philadelphians as being somewhere beyond the moon. With several partners he bought eight hundred acres of land on the west side of where the Mississippi River begins and attempted to build a city there, naming it Nininger City in honor of one of his partners.

At about the same time, he began publishing the *Emigrant Aid Journal*, a magazine filled with helpful information for the hundreds of German, Swedes and Norwegians flooding into the region. Having spent his youngest years in Philadelphia, Donnelly could speak German haltingly, never really mastering its syntax, and probably mixing it with the Pennsylvania Dutch idiom common on the streets of the Quaker state.

The impressive masthead of Donnelly's *Journal* showed steamboats on the river racing like mad toward Nininger City and also pictured a grand metropolis surrounded by acres of waving wheat, covered wagons creaking into town. and railroads belching smoke over it all.

Nearby land purchased by him and his partners was sold at cost — about six dollars a lot — and only men who signed to settle on the property were accepted. No person could buy a lot unless he promised to start making improvements on it within six months and complete them within two years.

In five years, Nininger City was abustle; lots sold rapidly, and the *Emigrant Aid Journal* although showing only a marginal profit was coming off the press in thousands of copies. Donnelly's dream of a city where artistic and intellectual pursuits went hand in hand with agriculture and industry seemed to be coming true. A literary conclave named the *Atheneum Company* was formed as well as a musical society. Alongside articles reporting on these endeavors might be an account of how to make better butter, how to treat sick farm animals, how to maintain farm machinery, or perhaps a poem by John Greenleaf Whittier.

In 1857 Nininger City was at its highest, but in that year an economic crisis swept the nation; banks closed, factories shut down, and wheat, which couldn't be sold at any price, rotted in the fields. The depression reached into Nininger City, and adding to the distress, the Railroad (which Donnelly insisted should be spelled with a capital R), ignored Nininger City and chose to route its rails through nearby Hastings.

The Railroad was more enticing than culture, so residents in Nininger City picked up belongings and moved to Hastings or elsewhere. The *Journal* folded, and Donnelly's dream of a model metropolis was blown away quicker than a Minnesota whirlwind.

Donnelly was far from daunted. After the demise of his dream city, he turned to politics and as a Republican was elected lieutenant governor of Minnesota (1859–1863). Following that stint, he ran successfully for the U.S. Congress and served six terms in the House of Representatives.

After his years in the U.S. Congress, Donnelly directed his talents into writing and state politics. He was a state senator for four years (1883–1887), a state representative for one (1887–1888) and subsequently held one or the other of these offices almost until his death in 1901.

Following his U.S. Congressional terms, Donnelly became identified with other liberal Republicans, and as editor of the weekly *Monopolist* (1874–1879) and later the *Representative*, he trumpeted the disenchantments and discontents of the agrarian frontier.

It was during this time, too, that he produced most of his published books. *Atlantis*, the first one, was a huge financial success, selling in such numbers as to rescue its author from his dire financial situation. *Atlantis* was written in such charming style as to make the whole theory of a sunken island plausible; the public read it and believed they were getting a sound dose of archeology.

A year after publication of *Atlantis*, Donnelly came out with another page-turner: *Ragnarok: The Age of Fire and Gravel*. In this one, he theorized that in some remote time a gigantic comet composed of clay, gravel, silt, and sand collided with earth, leaving on it those elements. *Ragnarok* had large sales but could not equal its forerunner.

In this third book, *The Great Cryptogram*, Donnelly tried to show by means of an ingenious cipher that Francis Bacon wrote all of the works commonly attributed to Shakespeare. Donnelly also asserted audaciously and gave "proof" that Bacon probably wrote Marlowe's plays, Montaigne's essays, and Burton's *Anatomy of Melancholy*.[3]

Most literary critics at the time either ignored *The Great Cryptogram* or ridiculed it, but an uproar was begun which never entirely disappeared.

In the U.S. Congress, Donnelly was recognized as one of its most dynamic orators, and his books as well as his politics propelled him onto the lecture platform.

He made brief lecture tours in the United States and in England before deciding to write pure fiction, turning out three novels. Of these, *Caesar's Column: A Story of the Twentieth Century*, was the most popular. In it the author told of the collapse of civilization from class struggles and predicted the coming of such entities as dirigibles with aluminum bodies, poison gas in warfare, television, and other modern conveniences. The story basically was one of protest, for Donnelly was convinced that bankers and financiers were responsible for the country's ills.

As the 1880s began, aspiring politicians were meeting with only limited success in getting farmers to the polls. Abortive movements such as the Greenbacks and the Grange had almost disappeared; discontent, however, not only remained but had spread. Protest groups formed in the South, the Southwest, and the Northwest — all with members who pledged to fight "the encroachments of concentrated capital and the tyranny of monopoly; . . .. to oppose, in our respective political parties, the election of any candidate to office . . . who is not in sympathy with the farmers' interest."

Every conceivable gathering place — schoolhouse, church, rural town hall, open square or lush meadow — was thronged regularly with visiting speakers who came to preach to the choir. Visiting orators might differ in style, but the substance of their messages was common: money scarcity, high interest rates, exorbitant taxes, and the gouging practices of railroads.

An assortment of platform howlers offered only slightly different remedies for the widespread poverty. In Kansas, Mary E. Lease gave incendiary advice: "What you farmers need to do is raise less corn and more hell!"

James B. Weaver of Iowa voiced similar complaints in a more restrained manner. Weaver had practiced law and had served in the Union Army during the Civil War, rising from the rank of private to that of brevet brigadier general. He had been elected to the U.S. Congress as a Representative from the Greenback Party, and in 1880 that Party chose him as its presidential candidate. Defeated in his bid for the higher office by Republican James Abram Garfield, the moderate Weaver became an active member in the emerging Populist Party.

Despite Weaver's loss in the campaign for the presidency, discordant factions did win significant victories in the elections of 1880.

One winner, Jerry Simpson was an amiable man whom even political foes liked as a person. Simpson reached the U.S. House of Representatives by reminding Kansas farmers that in the year before the voting they had to let their corn go for thirteen or fourteen cents a bushel; when that harvest reached Chicago, grain speculators there got forty-five cents for the same corn. Simpson's election, however, can be attributed to a quirk rather than to his arguments or eloquence. Called the "Sockless Socrates of the Prairie," Simpson triumphed over his opponent William A. Pfeffer, a champion whisker-grower in the Midwest.

Simpson had been given his sobriquet during an earlier and unsuccessful run for the state legislature in Kansas. His opponent in that race was wealthier and better provided than he, and in a grass roots talk Simpson remarked that while his foe could easily afford to wear silk socks, he himself was hard-pressed even to buy a pair of them. A reporter covering the talk touched it up by asserting that indeed Simpson wore no socks. The barefoot boy is a stock figure in American sentiment, and the spice of humor in the moniker "Sockless" appealed to voters; largely that nickname alone is Simpson's political record.

Another giving voice to the plight of farmers was Benjamin Tillman of South Carolina. Tillman with his one eye and unruly shock of hair led onslaughts against black Carolinians who dared to vote for Republicans. As governor and later as a U.S. senator, he shouted his hate for "plutocrats," and with equal passion he tried to disenfranchise blacks. Vehement on the platform and sometimes carried away by his own rhetoric, Tillman is remembered mainly because of the nickname "Pitchfork," given when he yelled to an audience he would like nothing better "than to stick a pitchfork into the fat ribs of Grover Cleveland."[4]

Most demagogic of the collection of Populist orators for the Peoples' Party was Tom Watson of Georgia. Watson's father owned forty-five slaves and 1300 acres of fertile Georgia farmland, putting him in the top six per cent on the economic scale. A twice-wounded Confederate soldier, the father came back from the Civil War to find his labor force gone, his livestock destroyed, fields overgrown with weeds, and log fences torn down and burned for home fires. He had lost everything before his son reached teen age; the once upper-class family had fallen to the level of the poorest whites.

In consequence of their straits, Tom Watson grew up not as one of the idle rich; he could plow and did plow a furrow as straight as any man in the county. Somehow Tom Watson managed to get enough money to attend two years of college. Then he taught school for two years, earning enough to enable him to get a law degree. He entered politics and served in the Georgia legislature before winning a seat in the U.S. House of Representatives.

Watson was poisonously anti-Catholic, anti-Semitic, and anti-Negro ("Negro" was the prevalent term during the lives of the individuals portrayed in this book. The words "black" or "colored" would have been pejorative.) He gained his political strength from championship of the small farmer.

In Congress and from platforms throughout Dixie he leveled his salvoes at "millionaire plunderers" and boasted that he was the only candidate that stood squarely for white supremacy.[5]

Ignatius Donnelly was politically linked with such extremists, and some might dismiss him as a crank, but no one could rightly call him a demagogue. He never pitted one race against another. He spoke for those who for one reason or another — language difficulties, lack of money, no training, no skills, or facing social discrimination — were locked out of promised American opportunities.

The age was saturated with evangelical fervor. Members of the cloth were always available to intone prayers and liturgies as reverent mingled with irreverent in crowds of workers and farmers gathered to hear itinerant preachers who with practiced eloquence would lace their protest themes with holy scripture. A leading labor leader, later excommunicated for his vigorous defense of the Knights of Labor, described Christ as "an evicted peasant, who came to preach a gospel of liberty to the slave, of justice to the poor, of paying the full hire to the workman."

Led by Frances E. Willard, the *Woman's Christian Temperance Union* (WCTU), the largest women's group in the nation at the time, claimed its work to close down saloons, improve prison conditions, shelter prostitutes, and support labor unions for women were all examples of "God in politics."

Nor did social gospelers stay out of the fray. Henry George predicted that a Single Tax on unimproved land, proposed in his 1879 epic *Progress and Poverty*, would bring "the culmination of Christianity — the City of God on earth — with its walls of jasper and its gates of pearl."[6]

George's thesis, i.e., *that the economic rent of land and the unearned increase in land values profited a few individuals rather than the community, thereby making the land valuable*, engendered great support but also elicited considerable refutation from serious thinkers. Clear presentation and a rational approach backed with recognized data made his book, *Progress and Poverty*, tremendously popular, and it sold millions of copies all over the world. Nor has the book been forgotten; even today George's theories influence tax legislation in the U.S., Australia, Canada, and certain nations of Western Europe.

Every faction harbors moderates as well as extremists, and agrarian protest groups in the second half of the nineteenth century were no exceptions. On the wildest fringes of the period's protestors was William Hope Harvey, a real estate operator who published a little, yellow-backed volume he entitled *Coin's Financial School.*

In it Harvey described a school planned and taught by "Professor Coin," a pseudonym for himself. The front cover of *Coin's Financial School* showed a big blackboard beside which stood *Professor Coin* in dress suit and silk hat. Throughout the book the *Professor* appears lecturing in the school carrying his name. According to author Harvey, the school attracted well-known merchants, bankers, and journalists who went away impressed with what they learned.

Most of Harvey's book is in dialogue, and the *Professor* through question-and-answer methods presents what he claims are patent failings in common understanding of economics. For example, when asked how two different metals, gold and silver, could remain at a fixed ratio to each other and also have the same commercial value, *Professor Coin* answers, "That is a common fallacy. All commercial values are regulated by supply and demand. If the demand for a particular commodity is rising and the supply does not increase, the commercial value will continue to rise." That response was enough to draw applause from the titans of business and industry in *Coin's* imaginary class.

Illustrations in the book were so simple that even the dimmest-witted could not fail to grasp the idea. One picture showed the head of an average business man; the head is filled with wires, cogs, and wheels behind which stands a man with his hand on a lever, ready to start the machinery. The single word *Banker* identifies the man.

An even more graphic illustration is labeled *Bimetallism*, and it shows factories belching smoke, a happy workman receiving his dinner pail from his robust, well-fed daughter. To the right of this pleasant scene is a ghastly one — *Monometallism* — factories that are shut, buzzards in the air, and human skeletons tottering in the foreground.

Gullible readers believed Harvey was reporting not fantasy but truths. He wrote that in his class were such successful figures as Leander McCormick, Phil D. Armour, and Marshall Field — not fact but another concoction of Harvey's fiction. *Coin's Financial School* sold for twenty-five cents and rolled off the presses in hundred-thousand lots. One writer estimated that more than four million copies of it were sold.[7]

Ignatius Donnelly was a contemporary of such extremists as Harvey, Watson, and Tillman, and he shared their complaints against the prevailing economic system, but his opposition was more rational. The Republicanism which he adopted for much of his adult life may have been moderated by his initial political leaning towards the Democrats. His first attraction was from the Democratic Party, and he ran with backing from that party in an unsuccessful bid to return to the House of Representatives. Yet the state and federal offices he held were gained under Republican banners.

As a young, impecunious lawyer in Philadelphia, Donnelly went along with those who regarded Whigs as aristocratic and hostile toward all immigrants — a cause which he adopted very early. At about the same time, the rise of the Know-Nothing Party and its satellites with their open prejudices made Democrats and their liberalism all the more appealing to the young idealist.

In July, 1855, Donnelly gave a speech on immigration to a Democratic County Assembly arguing that America with its vast lands and varied cultures was broad enough to absorb all the oppressed people of Europe and weld them into a democratic whole. The next year he offered John C. Breckinridge, destined to become leader of Southern Democrats who had split from Northern ones, all his support. Donnelly predicted the Republican Party would deteriorate after the election; then he added a further slap:

> The abolitionists will be as before, exalting the black over the white. The Know-Nothing will be once more holding his midnight council over the Irish and the Dutchman. The Yankee adventurer will return again to his peddling or his lecturing.[8]

Two years after firing this blast, Donnelly forsook his Democratic leaning and declared he had voted Republican! It was a flimsy alliance which would melt in political infighting, but Donnelly would be identified more or less with Republicans until his death forty-four years later.

After 1857, Donnelly's pronouncements grew increasingly reformist as he continued to deplore railroad excesses and capitalist gouging. Yet he was able to avoid the racial controversies that tarred the era.

At the close of the Civil War, radical Republicans wanted to provide political equality for all Negroes. In those times *Negro* or *Colored* were accepted; the term Black would have been pejorative. Underlying the stated pronouncements on race was a widespread belief that Negroes lacked sufficient intelligence for judgment and democracy. Donnelly supported President Lincoln's reconstruction program but repeatedly emphasized the need to educate the recently freed slaves. In opposition to Donnelly's views were radicals in the House, who adamantly stood alongside Speaker Thaddeus Stevens, embittered and dedicated foe of enfranchisement for freed Negroes.

There were not many Negroes in Minnesota in 1865, but Donnelly returned to Minnesota from Washington to stump the state pleading his case for Negro suffrage. Earlier that year when Republicans had held their state convention, he had persuaded fellow delegates to put in their plank a principle giving Negroes the right to vote. In consequence, a suffrage amendment was on the Minnesota ballot in the election that fall. Notwithstanding Donnelly's and his cohorts' efforts, the amendment failed; yet Donnelly remained inflexible on Negro rights.

Donnelly torpedoed the *vox populi* with his own speculation:

> I challenge the history of the past to produce a single instance where a revolution has occurred under equal laws in the attempt of any class to rise above the level of common rights to oppress any other portion of the population. The selfishness of human nature is not capable of any such effort. But I challenge the historian to point to a single community where unjust laws did not sooner or later result in wars and turbulence. . . .
>
> If it is true as argued by some that the history of the world shows that the Negro [sic] belongs to an inferior race, that he is unfitted to compete

with the white man in the desperate struggle for life, the more reason is
here why he should be protected by equal laws.[9]

At the time he made this speculation, Donnelly was no newcomer to the
cause of equal rights and laws. His production of the *Emigrant Aid Journal*
stemmed from his sympathy with those who because of language difficulties or lack of education were locked out of society's mainstream. In 1865
when Negro suffrage was on the Minnesota ballot, he spoke eloquently and
frequently in favor of enfranchisement. He vehemently rebutted those who
said the Negro lacked sufficient intelligence for voting, and at the same time
he urged a program of widespread education for freed slaves.

As a novice congressman in 1884, he led a fight against the corruption-
ridden Indian Office, where bribery and exploitations were common practices. It was a time when an Indian agent appointed by the U.S. Government
at a salary of $1,500 per year could retire after four years in office with a
$50,000 bank account. No wonder so many sought the lucrative appoint-
ment! Donnelly came out of the Congressional investigation of Indian affairs
as a champion who had thwarted fraud and chicanery.

Often allied politically with leaders from Dixieland who regarded blacks
as an inferior race, Donnelly never shared their views. His attitude towards
Indians, Negroes, and Jews — indeed any group outside of mainstream society — were shaped because he abhorred discrimination, and he sympathized
with those who suffered from it.

He deplored the readiness of intelligent people in the South to compromise their principles in order to retain political and economic power, and
he struck hard at the ingrained Southern mind in its dealing with race: its
inability to apply usual judgments of good and evil, of moral or immoral, of
legal and illegal.

Donnelly's attitude toward blacks can best be gleaned from *Doctor Huguet*, a fantasy he wrote in the autumn of 1890. The book never reached the
popularity of his other writings, perhaps because of its themes, but more
likely because it was too esoteric.

The main character, Dr. Huguet, was a white Southern physician infat-
uated with a lovely Southern lady who encouraged him to keep secret his
views on racial equality; they were too radical for the time and region. To
narrate those views, Donnelly through transfiguration places them in the
body of the coarsest and most brutal Negro imaginable. Gradually, Dr. Huguet's morals and behavior increasingly feed into the habits of this formerly
brutal Negro, who gradually reforms into a worthy character.

Acceptance of the book was disappointing, but it kindled a flame in several readers. The feeling was expressed by one Negro physician in Little Rock, Arkansas, who declared, "Any white man who can afford to speak out in such unmistakable terms for a race who have so little to reward him, is to be praised by every colored man."

Burton A. Aylesworth, President of Drake University in Des Moines offered similar praise and wrote Donnelly that the book,

> . . . assaults prejudice like a tempest. . . . Every black man has been other than he was; since I read Dr. Huguet, I am not the same myself.[10]

Donnelly's attitude toward Jews was ambivalent and cannot be easily explained. Some critics would never forgive him for statements he made during the critical months of Minnesota politics in 1893-1894. The state, famous for its frigid winters, had ordinary citizens in those years who were alarmed over rising prices of the much needed coal. From numerous platforms, Donnelly condemned price fixing by "coal combines" and presented his demands for anti-monopoly legislation. His message was manna to thousands of Minnesotans. Almost at the rise of the People's Party in 1892, Donnelly made demonetizing of silver (i.e., stopping the use of silver as a monetary standard) a genuine campaign issue. In a signed article he defended assertions of a conspiracy on the part of English bankers, including the Jewish House of Rothschild, who were interested in having U.S. bonds repaid in gold so that they could reap enormous profits.

A year later in the summer of 1893, President Grover Cleveland summoned a special session of Congress for the purpose of considering repeal of the Sherman Silver Purchase Law, and just prior to that session the American Bimetallic League held a conference in Chicago. Numerous Republicans and Democrats attended, but the most aggressive speeches were made by members of the People's Party. Governor Davis H. Waite of Colorado won the sobriquet "Bloody Bridles" when he shouted, "It is better, infinitely better . . . rather than that our liberties should be destroyed by tyranny . . . that we should wade through seas of blood — yea, blood to the horses' bridles."

Representing the People's Party also, Donnelly in his speech was not so vehement, but in denouncing the demonetization of silver he took a swipe at the alleged conspiracy of Jews and declared, "The Constitution should not be blotted out or become a weapon in the hands of the European Rothschilds."[11] Donnelly's critics never forgave him for that reference.

In 1894, the nation was shaken by the Pullman strike in Chicago. The American Railway Union called for a boycott of all Pullman cars, and when owner George Pullman refused offers of arbitration, the strike spread over almost the entire Middle and Far West. Despite protests from Illinois Governor John P. Altgeld, the federal government sent in troops to quell the disorder.

As the Pullman strike approached its climax, delegates from the Minnesota branch of the People's Party were gathering in Minneapolis for their state convention, and Donnelly was called upon to give the keynote address. In his talk, he placed responsibility for the strike upon corporate actions and the intransigence of owner George Pullman.

In ill health and still greatly upset by the recent death of his wife Kate, Donnelly nevertheless drew wild applause as he praised the American Railway Union and expressed hope that its members would stand by the People's Party.

Delegates at the convention chose Sidney M. Owen as its candidate for the Minnesota governorship, and as the fall campaign mounted to greater intensity, Donnelly's speeches in behalf of the Party grew more intemperate. In hammering away at financial conspiracies, he gave more ammunition to those who accused him of anti-Semitism when he referred despairingly to "Jewish money lenders."

He tried to explain that he did not blame Jews for becoming gold traders, and he pointed out that anti-Semite outbreaks in Europe, particularly in Germany, were the result of actions by a few wealthy Jews. Donnelly declared, "We (the People's Party) do not advocate another Spanish Inquisition, but we do advocate that Jews should get out of the gold bondage which now is destroying the human race."

The damage was done and could not be easily repaired, although Donnelly tried to do so a week later when he wrote an article insisting he did not mean to hurt anyone. Furthermore, he added:

> A plutocratic Jew is no worse than a plutocratic Christian — in fact he is half as bad, for the Jew for nearly 2,000 years has been proscribed, persecuted, hunted down; fenced into corners of towns, pelted and stoned by ignorant populations when Jews were preserving the knowledge of the one true God in the midst of an idolatrous and degraded world.

> We are fighting Plutocracy not because it is Jewish or Christian but because it is Plutocracy... We would be sorry to be understood as saying one word that would pander to prejudice against any man because of his race, religion, nationality, or color.[12]

Donnelly took frequent shots at those who interpreted criticisms of monopolies as being anti-Semitic, and choosing humor to ridicule such charges he liked to use the following anecdote:

> *There was a New York rowdy who knocked down a poor Jew.*
> *The Jew asked, "Why did you do that?"*
> *The rowdy replied, "Because you Jews killed Christ."*
> *"But that was 1800 years ago," replied the Jew.*
> *"It don't matter," said the roughneck. "I only heard about it last night."*[13]

The record will show that Donnelly's attitude toward Jews was inconsistent; at times he placed blame for financial distress upon Jewish financiers, but increasingly he spoke in defense of Jews as people like all others and blasted persons attacking them.

In the last years of his life, Donnelly deplored the wave of anti-Semitism that swept Europe and the United States following the Dreyfus hullabaloo in France. At that time in New York City, elderly Jews were abused in a series of "beard-pulling" incidents, and Donnelly condemned the outrage in no uncertain terms. Then in a subsequent article penned for the *Representative*, he wrote:

> The Jews are not all plutocrats. A large majority of them are the poorest people in the world. The half-starved workers in the sweat shops of London, Berlin, and New York are mostly Hebrews... It is inexplicable that a Christian people, worshipping a Jew, the son of a Jewess, should entertain such terrible bigotry against the people of his race.[14]

No one can be certain whether Donnelly's efforts to explain the plight of Jews was political posturing or sincere sympathy, but there is no doubt his written and spoken words about Jews softened with his advancing age.

Following his defeat in the election of 1884, Donnelly expected to be awarded patronage from the victorious Democrats. He had waged a valiant campaign backed by dissident Democrats. Although he had not declared himself a Democrat and had not supported the faction pushing for the election of the victorious Grover Cleveland, he first hoped to be appointed to some lucrative position, perhaps a lifetime judgeship or the United States general surveyor for the State of Minnesota.

Determined to obtain patronage, following Cleveland's inauguration, Donnelly went to Washington to join the crowd of office seekers. His friend William Vilas had been named postmaster general in the new administration and was a powerful link to the new President.

Vilas and Donnelly dined together and during that meeting Vilas agreed to arrange for Donnelly to meet with President Cleveland. Party politics back in Minnesota were at high boil, and Patrick Kelly, leader of conservative Democrats there, was opposed to Donnelly but had been put in charge of patronage for applicants from that state. Understandably, President Cleveland was circumspect in whatever assurances he may have given Donnelly.

Donnelly learned from Vilas that any position offered first had to have an endorsement from Kelly. In a note to Donnelly, Kelly responded: "I will be glad to assist you in obtaining a mission abroad should you desire it."

Donnelly was humiliated; his political support which he valued so highly had not been appreciated by the victorious Democrats. He fumed that he was not qualified for a small office at home but was good enough to represent the nation in lands overseas. He rejected the offer, for in his judgment accepting it would be surrendering and yielding his political leadership to his rival Patrick Kelly.

Friendship between Donnelly and William Vilas began to sour soon afterwards, and in June, Donnelly would enter a judgment in his diary:

> The RR & robber interest is [*sic*] all against me, and it is very potent. Vilas who professed great friendship is a cold-blooded politician & trickster & tool of Kelly.[15]

Remaining very active in politics, Donnelly was among a group of disenchanted persons who in 1892 met in St. Louis and launched the People's Party. At that meeting the eight hundred and sixty attendees included office holders, representatives from labor and trade union groups, farmers, and spokesmen for western intellectuals. They chose Ignatius Donnelly to draft the platform, and in the opening paragraphs of his preamble, he wrote:

> We meet in the midst of a nation brought to the verge of moral, political, and material ruin. . . The fruits of the toil of millions are boldly stolen to build up colossal fortunes for a few . . . Silver, which has been accepted as coin since the dawn of history has been demonetized to add to the purchasing power of gold by decreasing the value of all forms of property as well as human labor; and the supply of currency is purposely abridged to fatten usurers, bankrupt enterprise, and enslave industry.[16]

Four years later when Democrats met for their nominating convention in Chicago, the People's Party faction had weakened but was still strong enough to wield considerable influence. Even before the first gavel fell at the Chicago Coliseum, the convention had turned into a quarrelsome, disorderly affair. The dominant conservative "Bourbon Democrats" were under attacks from the party's more liberal wing — a mottled group that had chosen the silver issue as a device to disassociate itself from the Cleveland administration.

Donnelly, leader of the People's Party and acknowledged as its best orator, was chosen chairman of the platform committee — a committee which prepared a platform that would become a blueprint for the future. Donnelly, more than any other single delegate drafted the document, charting a course away from the *laissez-faire* policies of the past and setting forth principles which have been tenets of the Democratic Party ever since. The document called for government to control the money supply and take a more regulatory role in business and finance, redistribute wealth and power in America, tax the rich, and defend labor and small farmers against corporate aggressions.

The Chicago platform was an act of protest and change. Never before had delegates in nominating convention repudiated an incumbent president of their own party. The issues for which Democrats fought in 1896 led the party toward the New Freedom of Wilson, the New Deal of Franklin Roosevelt, and the Great Society of Lyndon Johnson yet to come. The 1896 platform offered a program aimed at redistributing America's wealth and political control in America. In rhetoric, at least, the Democratic Party has not retreated.

Donnelly's drafts brought horrible fear to most conservatives, for the documents he prepared called for the abolition of privately owned national banks and the establishment of postal savings banks. He was among the first to urge a law so that the president, vice president, and senators would be elected by direct vote of citizens. He aimed for a redistribution of America's wealth by raising income and inheritance taxes. He asked for universal suffrage, for more regulation of railroads and telegraph companies, more restrictions on general practices of business corporations, and a national law setting up an eight-hour working day for employees of industrial concerns.

By 1896 Donnelly's health was jeopardized by age, flu, and despondency growing from political defeats, and the death of his beloved wife Kate. The convention captured that year by William Jennings Bryan was the last hurrah for Ignatius Donnelly.

His life had been kaleidoscopic and his interests more intense than profound as he meandered through the fields of politics, history, literature, and philosophy. From rostrums and editorials he had fired salvoes that were adroit and clever but full of sophistries; no one could make the worse appear as the better reasoning.

Perhaps somewhere in his psychological make-up was an errant gene that drove him to favor the underdog; the predilection was evident. He joined rump parties such as the Radical Republicans, Anti-Monopoly, Democratic, Grange, Greenback, and the People's or Populist Party in part because they challenged established leadership. For similar reasons, he was unorthodox on religious matters.

There is little doubt that Donnelly was a braggart who talked convincingly on any subject dealing with politics. His fame as an orator echoed through halls of Congress and throughout the Midwest. Everyone recognized his short, plump figure, smooth-shaven face, tawny hair, and genial smile. Outside of politics, people liked him, and neighbors rarely deserted him even at the ballot box. He was at his best in leveling denunciations of opponents or lauding his supporters.

Ignatius Donnelly died on the first day of 1901, and on the occasion of his death supporters and political foes recognized that he had been "the greatest orator of Populism" — an orator who had broken the lance for every reform clause U.S. citizens had known during post-Civil War Republicanism.

Chronology of Ignatius Donnelly

Ignatius Donnelly born in Philadelphia, November 3, 1831.

Elementary High School and legal training in Philadelphia, 1837–1851.

Philadelphia lawyer, 1852–1856.

Married Kate McCaffrey, September 1855.

Moved to Minnesota in 1856.

Professed Democrat 1856; became Republican, 1858.

With partners, bought land to build Nininger City, 1857–1858.

Began publication of the *Emigrant Aid Journal*, 1856.

Lieutenant Governor and/or Acting Governor of Minnesota, 1859–1861.

Republican, U.S. Congressman, 1863–1869.

Defeated as Congressional candidate of the People's Party, 1870.

Led Anti-Monopoly Democratic Coalition Party, 1874–1878.

Wrote *Atlantis* and *Ragnarok*, 1881–1883.

Defeated as Democrat in Run for Congress, 1884.

Great Cryptogram Imbroglio, 1884–1889.

Failed under Farmers' Alliance to Win Governorship of MN, 1888.

Wrote *Caesar's Column* (Fiction), 1889–1890.

Published his controversial book, *Dr. Huguet*, 1891.

Led Formation of People's Party, 1891–1892.

Wrote basic principles for People's Party, 1892.

Unsuccessful Run for Minnesota Governorship under People's Party, 1892.

Wife Kate died in June, 1894.

Married Marian Olive Hansen in 1898.

Vice Presidential candidate of People's Party in 1900.

Died January 1, 1901.

CHAPTER 2. THEODORE ROOSEVELT: PATRICIAN RENEGADE

Autumn of 1858 was historic in the United States. There had been rejection of the Lecompton Constitution by Kansas voters in whose state, at the time, slavery was legal by virtue of the Dred Scott decision; practically, it was excluded though because of free soil domination. Also in that year, Abraham Lincoln and Stephen Douglas were traversing Illinois engaging in seven debates covering the slavery controversy and its impact on politics, law, and government.

Another event of interest at the time to only friends and family circle occurred in a brownstone home on East Twentieth Street in New York City early in the evening of October 27, 1858. In that sumptuous, five-story home, Mittie Bulloch Roosevelt gave birth to her second child, her first son, who would be christened Theodore Roosevelt, Jr. An adoring grandmother said the infant was "as sweet and pretty a young baby as I've ever seen," but the mother, despite her charm and loving disposition, spoke with Southern frankness and declared her newborn looked like a "terrapin."[1]

After the baby had reached adulthood and had been nominated for the vice presidency of the United States, Mark Hanna, National Chairman of the Republican Party, growled to fellow party members, "Don't you realize there is only one life between this madman and the presidency?" Other critics were no less restrained. James Wadsworth, asserted that TR was "unreliable, a faker, and a humbug." The editor of the *St. Louis Censor* assessed him as "the most dangerous foe to human liberty that has ever set foot on American soil." Hanna went further in denunciations and claimed Roosevelt was "drunk with power;" even Woodrow Wilson agreed by remarking, "He is the most dangerous man of the age," Mark Twain weighed in with, "The President is clearly insane . . . and insanest upon war and its supreme glories."[2]

As every occupant of the nation's highest elective office has attested, a person in public life is certain to draw praise as well as criticism. Of all who achieved the position, very few sparked such a range of extremes as did this twenty-fifth President. Moreover, no President was ever such a favorable target for cartoonists. They had field days in drawing figures of the medium tall, heavy set muscular man with a dazzling set of teeth and rimless pince-nez spectacles. The teeth and spectacles were such identifiable icons that envelopes ornamented only with them sometimes were delivered to the White House.

TR had plenty of critics, but he had admirers who went to equal extremes. British author H. G. Wells wrote that Roosevelt had "the most vigorous brain in a conspicuously responsible position in all the world."[3]

Few Americans have been born into such a balanced home environment as was Theodore Roosevelt. Theodore was called Teedie in his youth, and from the earliest days of New York his ancestors had ascended the social scale to become manufacturers, engineers, or prominent bankers. Industrious, talented, and honest, the family had amassed a comfortable fortune by the mid-1800s. Teedie's paternal ancestors preferred the security of commerce to the glamour of politics. His grandfather, Cornelius van Schaack Roosevelt, was said to be worth more than half a million dollars when the average daily wage was fifty to seventy-five cents.

Mittie Bulloch, Teedie's mother, having come from a line of distinguished politicians in the South, including one who was the first president of revolutionary Georgia, brought an element of feminine humor and taste into the family. From his father, Theodore most likely absorbed the rewards of privilege and the responsibilities of charity, but it is also probable that it was Mittie who bequeathed him flair, vigor, and his unconquerable egotism.

Throughout childhood, Theodore Roosevelt was a chronic invalid, suffering from frequent and baffling attacks of asthma. Confined indoors by ill-health, he wheezed restlessly from room to room and turned to reading: legends, myths, and then histories, biographies, anything he could lay hands upon. From readings, he gathered an amazing amount of information about natural history and augmented it by close observations whenever possible of the flora and fauna around his father's several homes in New York.

Teedie was ten years old when his father and mother took him, sisters Bamie and Connie, as well as brother Elly on a lengthy trip to Europe — an excursion which lasted for 377 days. The family visited the Netherlands and northern Germany, traveled the Rhine, glided in gondolas through the waterways of Venice, and then came back west to climb the Alps. At times, crippling asthmatic attacks kept Teedie down, but he would recover enough to accompany his father on treks which other family members judged were beyond their own energy or capability. All of this at a time when most American boys his age were just beginning to work in fields, sell newspapers, or shine shoes for 5 or 10 cents per hour.

In the fall of 1876, two months before his eighteenth birthday, Theodore Roosevelt enrolled at Harvard. Theodore, Sr. died in the following year, and Theodore Jr. upon his father's death inherited $125,000, learning also that he would get $62,000 more when his mother died.

At Harvard, Teedie lived well, spending more each year than the college president, Charles Eliot, earned in annual income. Yet TR's expenses were only on a par with those of Richard Welling, Harry Minot, Henry Cabot Lodge, Robert Bacon, Dick Saltonstall, and other wealthy New York boys or scions from Boston Brahmins.

Near the end of his second decade, TR was invited to Dick Saltonstall's home on Chestnut Hill near Boston, and on that visit he met Alice Hathaway Lee. It was October, 1878, and within a month TR vowed to himself that Alice was the girl he was going to marry. For the impetuous swain their courtship was agonizingly slow, and it was not until January, 1880, that Alice accepted his proposal.

In June of that year Theodore graduated from Harvard College with a B.A. *magna cum laude*, twenty-first in a class of one hundred and seventy seven. He and brother Ellie made a quick hunting trip through Illinois, Iowa, and Minnesota that summer, and then near the end of September, TR returned to New York City where his intended bride was making plans for the wedding.

The event took place in Brookline, Massachusetts, the following October, and soon afterwards the newlyweds set up residence at 6 West 57th St. in New York City. Theodore enrolled and began attending classes at the Columbia Law School in the city.

It was a busy time for the young couple with many evenings spent with friends in some of New York's finest drawing rooms, church on Sundays, and rides through the parks as well as Theodore's five full days each week at the law school. One wonders how he managed to find time to visit Morton Hall.

Morton Hall was a decided contrast to the swells usually attended by Theodore and Alice. It was really nothing but a barn-sized chamber over a store, yet it served as headquarters for the Twenty-first District Republican Association. Here cheap lawyers, saloonkeepers, streetcar conductors, and ward heelers — mostly Irish — gathered for political meetings once or twice a month.

As soon as the last afternoon class at Columbia ended and well before the dinner hour at home, young Theodore would dash across Fifth Avenue, round the corner of 59th St. and up the shabby flight of stairs to Morton Hall. In his expensive clothes, with pince-nez tied to a string leading to his lapel, side-whiskers, and cultured accents, he was indeed a *rara avis*, not welcomed at first, but he came back again and again and eventually was accepted as a member.

When family members learned Theodore was regularly attending meetings in Morton Hall, they were appalled. His father's friends assured him that gentlemen with "upbringing" simply did not traffic with professional politicians. Gentlemen might contribute campaign funds, of course, but to associate and mingle with the pros! That was beneath one's dignity!

TR responded with characteristic frankness:

> I answered that if this were so, it merely meant that the people I knew did not belong to the governing class, and that the other people did. . . I intended to be one of the governing class; if they proved too hard for me I supposed I would have to quit, but certainly I would not quit until I had made the effort to find out whether I really was too weak to hold my own in the rough and tumble.[4]

Within months after his initial attendance at Morton Hall, TR began taking an active role in party politics, attending primary gatherings in addition to regular meetings and working his way up into the executive committee of the Young Republicans.

There was a hiatus from politics beginning in May, 1881, when Theodore and Alice took a delayed honeymoon trip to Europe, visiting Ireland, Venice, and the Alps. There in the first week of August he successfully climbed the fifteen-thousand-foot Matterhorn to its top. He and his wife returned to America that September, and TR finished writing of *The Naval War of 1812*.

Reviewing his third trip abroad in twelve years, TR wrote Bill Sewall:

> I have enjoyed it greatly, yet the more I see the better satisfied I am that I am an American; free born and free bred, where I acknowledge no superior except for his own worth, or my inferior for his own demerit.[5]

In October, 1881, political allies at Morton Hall nominated Theodore Roosevelt for the State Assembly. Friends, relatives, and Republicans disgruntled with entrenched leaders rallied to his candidacy, and the results in the November election showed his triumph with a sizeable majority.

As an incoming assemblyman, TR arrived in Albany on a cold, windy day the second of January, 1882. At twenty-three years of age, he was the youngest man in the legislature. He was depressed by the slowness of actions in that legislative body and complained to close friends and relatives that he was not going to spend his life in politics. His protestations have to be taken with grains of salt, however, for from his first election until well after he lost his last, politics remained the North Star guiding his career.

There was a prolonged battle in the State Assembly over selection of a Speaker, a deadlock broken in February when the winner, Democratic nominee Charles Patterson, was chosen. The new Speaker awarded Roosevelt a position on the Committee of Cities. TR was pleased, and within a week of his appointment to the committee he introduced four bills: one to purify New York's water supply, another to upgrade its system for picking aldermen, a third to cancel all stocks and bonds in the city's "sinking fund," and a fourth to lighten the judicial burden on the Court of Appeals. Only one of these bills — the aldermen bill — ever achieved passage, but that fact did not deter TR. Determined to fight on, he saw himself as a knight in shining armor, facing the "black horse cavalry," his epithet for machine politicians.

As an acknowledged reformer in the Assembly at Albany, TR became more familiar with the extent of corruption and bribery in New York State politics. The first major speech in his long career was delivered to the Assembly on April 5, 1882, when he accused former State Attorney Hamilton

Ward and State Supreme Court Justice T. R. Westbrook of collaborating and engaging in fraudulent practices in order to obtain shares of stock in the giant Manhattan Elevated Railroad, a corporation owned by financier Jay Gould. TR identified Ward, Westbrook, and Gould by name, describing them as "sharks" and "swindlers." Such direct language had not been heard in the Assembly prior to that time, and regulars were shocked as were even some of TR's supporters.

Debates over his call for impeachment were sensational and dragged on until May. It looked as if the young reformer had won enough votes to get his motion approved, but through last minute parliamentary maneuvers and a few bribes, three members who formerly had signed in favor of impeachment, switched their votes. The majority for impeachment was changed to a majority against it, and the chairman reported that Judge Westbrook had been merely "indiscreet," in trying to save the Manhattan Railroad from destruction.[6]

Westbrook and Ward had escaped from TR's fusillade at the last moment, but their venality had been exposed, and from that exposure his own political stature was on the rise. Often lampooned by opponents as that "dude from New York City," a group of reformers and idealists in the Republican Party began forming around him. Then early in 1883, a champion of the opposing party wanted to meet him.

Democrat Grover Cleveland, former mayor of Buffalo, had won the governorship with the largest plurality of votes in New York State's history up until that time. Taking office in January 1, 1883, the new governor asked Theodore Roosevelt to come to his office for a visit. The matter Governor Cleveland wanted to discuss with the rebel from the Assembly was reform in the Civil Service System.

In the previous year, reformers in the U.S. Congress had passed a measure making 10% of all federal jobs subject to written examinations. In their Albany discussion, both Governor Cleveland and TR noted the federal Act and agreed that the "spoils system" for awarding civil service posts ought to be abandoned and replaced by requiring written examinations for all such appointments. Furthermore, competent and honest men in civil service posts should remain there irrespective of the ins and outs of government.

Such ideas, of course, were anathema to machine politicians who insisted that handing out political plums was necessary for successful administration. As a member of the State Assembly, TR's speeches flaying municipal corruption were ruthlessly non-partisan. In one talk, he named four aldermen as vote-sellers to Tammany Hall — the four individuals named were all Republicans. He concluded with an extreme statement declaring that if every Republican holding a municipal office were removed, "the party throughout the state and nation would be benefited rather than harmed."[7] Fellow reformers applauded his generalization, but regulars in the party, deciding they couldn't control the rebel, shied away from him.

When the second month of 1884 began, TR was very much involved in party struggles within the Assembly. Tuesdays through Fridays he would spend full days and nights in Albany. Late on Friday, he would board a train for the ride back to New York where he could enjoy a treasured week-end with his wife who was, at the time, in her ninth month of pregnancy. He also would manage to visit his mother Mittie, who was quite ill, suffering what appeared to be a lingering cold.

TR was in Albany attending an Assembly session on Tuesday, February 12th when his wife Alice went into labor. That night she gave birth to a baby girl, and the next morning while TR was accepting congratulations from his friends a second telegram arrived. Looking suddenly worn and tired, he rushed for the next train.

By the time TR reached his wife's bedside and took her in his arms, Alice barely knew who he was. He was there, holding her, a short time after midnight when he was told that if he wished to see his mother alive, he must come at once.

He rushed to Mittie's bedside, but his mother passed away at three o'clock in the morning. Doctors told TR she had died of typhoid fever. His wife Alice, suffering from Bright's Disease, lingered for eleven hours before dying at two o'clock the next afternoon.

The two persons he loved most in the world, dying within the same twenty four hours! No one could explain such a tragedy. Theodore would describe it as "God's will," or "fate, strange and terrible." His mother had been only forty-eight-years old, and his wife just twenty-two, her life barely begun; now both were gone.

There was no recourse except to lose himself in work, and TR tried to do that. Week after week throughout March and April, 1884, he shunted back and forth from Albany to his committee hearings on city matters in New York.

At the onset of June, Republicans arrived in Chicago to begin their nominating convention. James G. Blaine, named the "plumed knight" by Robert Ingersoll in an eloquent nominating speech eight years earlier, was the clear favorite. But some of Blaine's plumes had become bedraggled through exposures of men like Carl Schurz. Also, E. L. Godkin, and Henry Cabot Lodge--Republican stalwarts — talked openly of bolting the party if Blaine were the nominee.

Despite efforts of those who wanted to block his nomination, Blaine after several contentious votes was chosen by the delegates. A disappointed and frustrated Theodore Roosevelt went back to New York where he visited his sister Bamie, now caring for his six-month old daughter Alice. While in New York, TR responding to a reporter's question said that despite his failed opposition to Blaine, he still intended to vote the Republican ticket, adding,

> I did my best and got beaten... I am by inheritance a Republican, whatever good I have been able to accomplish in public life has been accomplished through the Republican Party. I have acted with it in the past and wish to act with it in the future... I am going back in a day or to my western ranches, as I do not expect to take part in the campaign this fall.[8]

The Democrats chose stolid Grover Cleveland, former mayor of Buffalo and then Governor of New York, as their standard bearer. Throughout that fall, Cleveland droned on about tariff matters and Civil Service Reform. Nearly all pundits saw inevitable victory for Republican James Blaine.

The campaign was in its final week when in New York a garrulous Presbyterian minister with Blaine standing by his side accused the Democratic party of representing "rum, Romanism, and rebellion." A smiling Blaine didn't change expressions, but since he said or did nothing to deny the *faux pas*, reporters and readers interpreted his silence as agreement. Within hours the insult had been telegraphed to every Democratic newspaper in the country; headlines and handbills amplified the allegation a thousand fold, and Blaine's support melted faster than snow in April sunshine. On November 4, 1884, Grover Cleveland, polling 23,005 more popular votes than Blaine, became the nation's first Democratic president in a quarter of a century.

The Bad Lands cattle boom had begun in the Dakota Territory a year earlier and was in its initial stage when TR had made his first visit and impetuously invested $14,000. The money was to buy 450 head of cattle, for like others, TR bought no land but was a squatter on free land offered by the federal government. The nearest settlement of any kind to the land TR chose was Medora, which eastern newspapers described as a "thriving, bustling" town with nearly a thousand people and a promising future. TR's intent was to let his cattle graze on the free land, and butcher the steers there in the Bad Lands beside the railroad. Thus he would avoid the cost of shipping the live animals all the way back to Chicago; new refrigerated box cars already had been demonstrated.

He called his first ranch The Maltese Cross and wrote Bamie that the outlook for making a business success of ranching was "very hopeful." The Maltese Cross was just south of Medora, and within several months TR took up more land for grazing thirty miles north of Medora, calling the addition Elkhorn.

It cannot be said that TR was a good businessman. His tendencies were to spend freely and invest in dubious enterprises on sudden impulse. Having grown up with wealth, he never knew what it meant to be without it; although there were times when his assets were perilously low. Yet the ranches gave him a vigorous life — a life he loved — long days in the saddle, chasing and branding steers, often sleeping on the ground near a smoldering campfire. In daytime, dust and heat might be terrific, and yet he might ride a hundred miles or more.

The untamed western lands were ideal for hunters, trappers, and sportsmen. TR was never a trapper, for he had too much compassion for animals to have them suffer in snares he himself had set. He was an inveterate hunter, however, and his western homeland offered buffalo, deer, antelope, and bears — black or grizzly. He was a paradox when it came to hunting, for he killed often and was inordinately proud of what he brought home. It was not at all unusual for men of his class to hunt big game, yet he had a code of personal morality which led him to scorn those who wasted game:

> I have nothing but contempt for the swinish game-butchers who hunt for hides and not for sport or actual food, and who murder the gravid foe and the spotted fawn with as little hesitation as they would kill a buck with ten points. No one who is not himself a sportsman and lover of nature can realize the intense indignation with which a true hunter sees these butchers at their brutal work of slaughtering the game, in season and out, for the sake of a few dollars which they are too lazy to earn in any other and more honest way.[9]

Amidst ranch work and hunting forays he somehow found time to write his impressions of western grandeur. His buoyancy of spirits and vigor of body rose dramatically, and never again would he be as strong in muscle and sinew as he was during 1884–1887 in the Bad Lands of the Dakota Territory.

Notwithstanding his enchantment with western life, TR was unable to keep away from New York for long. In slightly more than one year he made four trips from the west to New York where he could visit Bamie and "Baby Lee," the pet name he had bestowed on his infant daughter.

Politics was in his blood, and he never tried to get it out. When he left Dakota and went back east, he was pressured by Republicans to run for Mayor of New York City. Yielding to their persuasions, although almost commuting from west to east, he agreed and ran in the election of 1886. Odds were against him in that campaign, however.

Democrats nominated Abraham Hewitt, a wealthy man with moderate opinions. Hewitt had gained a large following among rank and file voters during the depression years of 1873–1878 when he kept his steel works open at a loss in order to safeguard jobs of his employees. Also, a new Labor party had been formed and sponsored the single-tax proponent Henry George, a man TR had met and liked but considered mainly "wind."

Both Hewitt and George were formidable opponents — the former an experienced and respected politician, and the latter offering a platform for the "disinherited class." George enchanted listeners gathered around him in New York's grimy streets by proclaiming, "What we are beginning here is the great American struggle for the ending of industrial slavery."

There was no doubt Hewitt would attract all but the most loyal of George's followers, and Hewitt ran a sober, dignified campaign although he expressed nervousness about the youth of Roosevelt.

To such concerns, his twenty-eight-year-old rival responded, "It has been objected that I am a boy, but I can only offer the time-honored reply, that years will cure me of it."

TR's innate optimism sustained him throughout an energetic campaign. He was not aloof but courteous toward opponents. Not until two or three days before votes were taken did he drop his friendliness and resort to name-calling: "Henry George," he said, "[was] a 'galled jade' and his cohorts nothing but 'peevish fossils.'" Hewitt and his backers were "the same old gang of thieves" who had robbed the city for years.

Despite TR's outbursts, observers would assess it as one of the most fairly-fought contests in the city's history. The three candidates were worthy ones; substantive issues were raised — social injustices by George, dangers of unionized politics by Hewitt, and municipal reform by Roosevelt.

Results of the city's election that fall were foreordained, for Democrats drew many moderate Republicans by making the most of the slogan: "A vote for Roosevelt is a vote for George."

Swarms of Republicans recalled that Roosevelt had gone against party regulars and had refused to support Blaine at the national level; also some feared the antics of this maverick from higher society. The final results of the ballot in 1886 made the Cowboy Candidate wince. Disenchanted party members defected to Hewitt; the vote results were unassailable: Hewitt 90,552, George 68,110, and Roosevelt 68,435.[10] TR was crushed temporarily, but his courage and perseverance were indestructible.

Coupled with his political defeat in New York, disaster from Mother Nature struck Roosevelt's Dakota holdings in the winter of 1886–1887 when the area suffered its worst weather on record. Blinding snows, relentless savage winds, freezing temperatures, and storm after storm swept the Great Plains. In areas around TR's ranches, families lost children or other members who froze to death within a few hundred yards of their homes. Snow was so deep in some places that cattle were buried alive, and at other times cattle desperate for shelter of any kind smashed their heads through ranch house windows.

Many ranchers lost everything they owned. TR estimated that he had invested at least $82,500 in cattle, cabins, and wages. When totaling his losses, he arrived at a figure in the order of $70,000, not counting interest his capital would have earned if invested elsewhere.[11]

TR sold his Dakota holdings and was in New York by the end of August, 1887. Back in the city of his birth, he was as busy as ever. His social schedule included innumerable dinner invitations, and on a personal front he resumed friendship with his childhood sweetheart Edith Carow. The two had corresponded while he was in the west, and 1886 had not ended before TR asked her to marry him. She accepted, but their engagement was kept secret for nearly a year before they married in London on December 2, 1886.

After their return to America, the newlyweds made their home at Sagamore Hill, near Oyster Bay, Long Island. TR remained active and outspoken in the Republican Party, and in 1889 President Benjamin Harrison appointed him a member of the U.S. Civil Service Commission. There were three members on the Commission, and Roosevelt was the newest, yet with his customary vigor he assumed leadership and for six years directed the Commission's battle against the spoils system.

He left the Commission in 1895 to become president of the Police Board of New York City where he faced a myriad of problems. The police force in the Empire State's biggest city, indeed the largest at the time in the nation, was rife with corruption, cronyism, and underworld connections. The vigorous, often flamboyant TR went at such challenges with the vigor he had shown in college, ranching, and earlier political campaigns. Entrenched politicians in both parties opposed him, yet in less than two years he succeeded in getting most political favoritism out of the New York City Police Force, thus making it a more neutral arm of municipal government. As the extremely active leader of the Board he bolstered morale by instituting a system of appointment and promotion by merit and by rigorous enforcement of existing laws regardless of political pressures. He had instituted a doctrine of respect for the law and restored a higher sense of honor and pride in those who were expected to enforce it. The biggest metropolitan newspaper, the *New York Times*, summarized, "The service he has rendered to the city is second to that of none."[12]

In February, 1898, the U.S. battleship *Maine blew up (or* was blown up — the cause has never been officially determined) in Havana harbor while the Cubans were in revolt against Spain, and TR, then Assistant Secretary of the Navy, seized upon the incident to strengthen U.S. naval forces. Hostilities with Spain broke out in April, and Roosevelt resigned from his cabinet position in order to join his friend Leonard Wood in organizing the first U.S. Volunteer Cavalry.

At the beginning of July, 1898, U.S. soldiers defeated outnumbered Spanish forces near Santiago, Cuba. The fighting at San Juan Hill was Theodore Roosevelt's stage, for he personally led his division in a rash but successful assault on an outpost called Kettle Hill. His Rough Riders, a diverse group that included western cowboys, college men, blacks, and native Americans, became the most celebrated regiment in the U. S. Cavalry. Roosevelt was 40 years old at the time, had been a state assemblyman, western rancher, a New York City Police Commissioner, and a candidate for mayor of that city. And no one can deny he knew the value of publicity.

When he joined American forces already in Cuba, he took with him a personal publicist, Richard Harding Davis. Colonel Roosevelt granted favors to Davis and to other journalists he liked, and largely from such reporters emerged a view that over emphasized his role. Moreover, Roosevelt's memoirs did the same to the extent that Mr. Dooley, the barroom pundit created by Peter Finley Dunne, remarked that those memoirs should have been called "Alone in Cuba."

Roosevelt's accounts as well as most newspaper stories of the San Juan Hill Battle are very calloused. When it came to war, TR was far from being compassionate. In private letters he had expressed concern that the war might end before he had a chance to get in on the fighting. Numerous military veterans writing in retrospect have attested to feeling numb over slaying enemies or that they regretted the necessary killing of other humans. Not so with Theodore Roosevelt; he had slight regard for life in battle, including his own. Heartless perhaps, but it was an attitude when coupled with his innate fortitude made him a genuine leader at San Juan.

Undeniably a hero there, he did not have all the banners himself. Military records confirm there were about 15,000 American troops participating in the San Juan Battle: 13,000 were white and 2,000 black. More than 200 American soldiers were killed in action, and 30 of those were from the four black Regular Army Regiments.

The records also claim that the San Juan episode was the first instance in which the U.S. Army used machine guns for fire in support of mobile offensive combat. The Gatling Detachment was ordered to move forward and support troops assaulting the blockhouse on San Juan Hill. Four to five men were needed to operate each of four machine guns in the Detachment, and when it came under heavy fire from Spanish regulars behind fortified positions or sharpshooters hiding in shrubbery, four men fell from wounds along with others succumbing to the intense heat. Nevertheless, it was the Gatlings which provided the covering fusillade that enabled ground troops led by the mounted Roosevelt to capture the outpost on Kettle Hill, prelude to San Juan itself. The Colonel said the "charge was great fun" and we "had a bully fight."

The fame TR gained from the exploit made him a national hero, and two weeks after the Rough Riders were mustered out of service, the Republican Party of New York nominated him for governor. He ran a campaign successful enough to win election by a scant majority and served as the Empire State's chief administrator for two years. His career as New York's governor marks the beginning of his active efforts to secure control and direction by government of great financial corporations.

In 1900, seasoned Republican politicians did not want Roosevelt to win re-election as governor, and in a ploy adopted to prevent that happening they managed to get him nominated for the vice presidency alongside the major candidate William McKinley. The election of 1900 put McKinley in the White House and installed Theodore Roosevelt as his vice president.

That election was a sweep for Republicans, and McKinley had served a mere six months before in Buffalo, New York, he was shot and died within days. Vice President Theodore Roosevelt took office immediately.

Every incoming president finds more problems than anticipated, and the 43-year-old Roosevelt was no exception. One of his most serious problems threatened the efficacy of democratic government — tenets on which the nation had been founded. Fifty years earlier the young country had survived a civil war which nearly tore it apart, and following that upheaval had come citizen unrest with protest groups such as the Populist and Greenback Parties. There had been a limited war with Spain over island possessions, but that had been concluded in favor of the United States.

On the economic front, the 1880s had seen the emergence of industrial pools and secret combinations of all sorts. By 1890 there were such pools in sugar, whiskey, tobacco, beef, cattle feed, wire nails, and even bicycles and electrical appliances. The Sherman Anti-Trust Act of 1890 was aimed at curbing such Trusts, or "conspiracies," but in truth it caused only a minor irritation.

Challenged as a monopoly in the State of New York, the American Sugar Refining Company appealed to the U.S. Supreme Court, which in a far-reaching decosopm showed that in reality the government had little or no interest in prosecuting Trusts.

The challenge facing Roosevelt upon taking the presidential oath of office in 1901 did not come from abroad nor from the unemployed or the oppressed but from the rich and powerful in his own country. The U.S. had expanded rapidly following the Civil War, and much of its growth was westward. Railroad engines chugged over Midwestern prairies and then over deserts all the way to California and Oregon on the West Coast. The expansion demanded steel, and workers to produce it, as well as ones to lay rails through miles of wasteland. Industrialists who put up factories to produce the steel and owners of the railroad corporations grew rich, powerful, and greedy — magnates able to influence elected officials and to shape political decisions.

These titans needed money to finance their ventures, however, and to get it they turned to bankers and lenders. Bankers and financiers in effect were revealed as the kingpins of the capitalist system.

In the East there was Edward H. Harriman, who had moved into capitalist ranks in 1887 when he became head of the Illinois Central Railroad. Under his guidance, the Illinois Central flourished, and the ambitious Wall Street gambler with strong backing from the Vanderbilts and their Standard Oil Trust moneys acquired one railroad after another.

In the northwestern tier of states, James J. Hill had built an industrial and agrarian empire. Hill's grain and lumber-carrying rail lines ran through Wisconsin, Minnesota, North and South Dakota, Wyoming, Montana, Oregon, and Washington, with no competition worthy of the name. Hill's chief holding was the Northern Pacific Railroad which dominated the northern half of the Great West.

Harriman and Hill were tycoons to be reckoned with, but neither they nor anyone else could match John Pierpont Morgan. He was the Colossus astride the financial world. In contrast with the Horatio Alger heroes of his time, Morgan had been born into a very affluent family. His grandfather had been first a proprietor of a coffee house and then a hotel keeper before organizing a canal company, steamboat lines, and finally a railroad — all of which returned him handsome profits. His son added to the family fortunes by becoming a prosperous dry goods merchant before engaging in foreign trade transactions, particularly in cotton. By the time of the American Civil War, Morgan and Company from Hartford, Connecticut was a firm recognized and respected by European industrial leaders.

John Pierpont Morgan was born on April 17, 1837 in his grandfather's house in Hartford, Connecticut. Young Pierpont — "Pip" as he was called throughout his boyhood — went to grammar school in Hartford, then a private boarding school in Connecticut before attending a Boston high school with exceptionally high standards. The family moved to London, and Pierpont for a short time went to a small college in Switzerland before transferring to the University of Gottingen in Germany. There was always plenty of money, and Pierpont was imbued with the New England faith in the breadth of education as well as thrift in business.

At the age of twenty, he began his business career as an accountant with a private bank in New York City. Each year thereafter, he increased the family fortunes. There were occasional losses but they were quickly erased by gambles which a prescient and a smart businessman like Pierpont was willing to take.

By 1879, J. P. Morgan was forty-two and without equal as the most powerful financier in America. In trusts and through interlocking directories he controlled the following railroads: the Chicago, Burlington and Quincy, the Southern Railway, Central of Georgia, Louisville and Nashville, Reading (Jersey Central, and Reading Coal and Iron), Erie, Hocking Valley, Lehigh Valley, Santa Fe, and St. Louis and San Francisco — some 55,555 miles of track worth over $3,000,000,000 in capital. [13]

Roosevelt was not yet President in May, 1901, when Morgan and Hill launched their idea of a "holding company." Hill's idea was to merge the corporations he controlled with those under Harriman, thus creating a union with capital so large nobody could buy it. Morgan, intrigued by the size of the project, jumped in, took it over, and formed the Northern Securities Corporation.

The new U.S. President was urged by party stalwarts to go slow in making changes, to be conservative and be safe, but that was not the nature of the reformist "Rough Rider." Moreover, here was growing public disenchantment whipped up by the "yellow" presses of Joseph Pulitzer and William Randolph Hearst, there was growing public disenchantment. Graphic accounts of palatial homes, private trains, disdain for the citizenry, and extravagant expenditures for costume balls, divorces, and scandals had soured the public on the millionaires.

The Northern Securities Corporation formed by Morgan and Hill was a wolf dressed in sheepskin. The two railroad kingdoms formerly controlled by Harriman and Hill were now one system consisting of more than 9,000 miles of railroad track, pooling resources, jointly selecting directors, and careful not to promote the interests of one system at the expense of the other.

In the White House, President Roosevelt had mixed emotions. He was a true descendant of the old aristocracy — now the brains and leaders of holding companies — but he had been bitten by the bugs of reformers such as followers of William Jennings Bryan and the young progressive governor of Wisconsin, Robert La Follette. TR had denounced the predations of Jay Gould, prototype for Hill and Harriman, as those "malefactors of great wealth," and now with the powers of the presidency behind him he was prepared to act.

In January, 1902, the State of Minnesota charged the Northern Securities Corporation with violation of its state statutes. Soon after that, President Roosevelt, acting with secrecy, ordered his Attorney General to prosecute the Northern Securities Corporation on grounds of violating the Sherman Anti-Trust Law. An infuriated J. P. Morgan went to the White House to protest and ask if the President meant "to attack my other interests."

TR gave him disingenuous assurance that no harm would befall him if he did no wrong. TR in effect had thrown a bomb into the financial world by bringing suit on behalf of the U.S. Government against the giant holding company. There was a great deal of legal wrangling and several trials were held before the U.S. Supreme Court finally ruled in favor of Roosevelt's case.

The Northern Securities Corporation was only the start of the conflict between President Roosevelt and large financial interests. Business leaders were convinced he was a destroyer bent on undermining private properties. TR rebutted such charges by asserting that he was not at all opposed to establishment of corporations but was concerned only with their wrong doings. With that interest uppermost in mind, he brought similar suits against U.S. Steel, the Standard Oil Company, the American Sugar Refining Company, and other powerful combinations.

Although born and bred to the purple, Theodore Roosevelt inveighed against "gluttons of privilege" and "malefactors of great wealth." The clubby set surrounding his youth and upbringing never forgave him. Despite the glory he would receive, he was considered a "traitor to his caste," a man who "should have been on the side of capital."[14]

On the legislative front, President Roosevelt sponsored laws which forbade railroads from giving rebates to favored shippers; he touted a Pure Foods bill that declared illegal the manufacturing, sale, or transportation of adulterated foods, drugs, medicines, or liquor. He initiated an Act providing for inspection of stockyards and packing-houses, and it was under his aegis that an Employers' Liability Act was adopted. No small wonder that press and public came to regard him as the great "Trust Buster."

Other moves which etched his role as a rebel within his political party as well as from popular social views were his actions regarding employers and labor. When a strike among miners in the anthracite coal industry brought the menace of public safety to the surface, Theodore Roosevelt, for the first time in the nation's history, asserted the right of the president to act as representative of the public in an industrial dispute.

Almost at the outset of his presidency, Theodore Roosevelt adopted a policy of conservation of the nation's natural resources. No actions during his presidential administrations aroused deeper public interest or sharper opposition than his efforts in behalf of conservation. Under his administrations the area of national forests was increased from 43 million to 194 million acres. Water resources were put under government control to prevent speculation and monopoly, and cattle raisers grazing herds on public lands were forced to pay for what they were getting.

TR's popularity was so great that when he ran for reelection in 1904, he received the largest majority ever given to a candidate up until that time.

In foreign affairs, Roosevelt's actions were swift, firm, and bold but never reckless. He had a better understanding of involutions in European politics than any President before him, and he was the first American President to grasp the part the Pacific would play in world history.

Although brilliantly assisted by John Hay and Elihu Root, TR was his own Secretary of State. With dogged persistence he tried to build the navy's power and instill in its practices appointments and promotions based on merit and qualifications rather than favoritism.

European powers had colonized islands in the West Indies and South America throughout most of the nineteenth century, and as early as the fourth quarter of that period, French entrepreneurs were exploring the possibilities of making an access across one or another of several isthmuses in Central America. Such a path would permit commercial vessels to transverse the two gigantic oceans without having to sail the long, torturous voyage around Cape Horn in South America.

In 1880 and for several years thereafter, Ferdinand de Lesseps, a noted French engineer, endeavored to raise enough capital to start the building of a canal. Indeed, de Lesseps came to America, was feted by financial barons in New York City and had a triumphant tour as far west as Pittsburgh during which he assured Americans his intended canal would be strictly a commercial enterprise unconnected in any way with the French government or its navy. Thus not only would the U.S. but Europe and the entire world benefit from greater seagoing exchanges of food and textiles.

Ground was broken in Central America, but disease, fever, and lack of skilled workers took their tolls. As costs for the project soared, French financiers turned away, and de Lesseps' grand scheme failed for lack of financing.

There were more years of fruitless negotiations over construction of a canal, and in 1903 when an opportunity arose for the United States to acquire rights to build such a structure, the forward-looking President Theodore Roosevelt jumped at it. Later, some historians would charge that he encouraged or even fomented a Panamanian revolution. One of America's most talented narrative historians, David McCullough, presents an extended discussion of the complex maneuvering preceding construction of the Panama Canal, but even McCulloch admits the question of Roosevelt's involvement is too murky for definite answers. It is known that on November 2, 1903, the day before the Panamanian Revolution took place, the commander of a U.S. gunboat, the Nashville, received secret orders to anchor near the harbor of Colon, Panama, where any landing of troops from Colombia could be observed. The orders read:

> Nashville, Care American Consul, Colon:
>
> Secret and confidential. Maintain free and uninterrupted transit. If interruption threatened by armed force, occupy line of the railroad to prevent landing of any armed force with hostile intent, either government or insurgent, either at Colon, Porto Bello, or other point.
>
> Send copy of instructions to senior officer present at Panama upon arrival of Boston. Have sent copy of instructions and have telegraphed Dixie to proceed with all possible dispatch from Kingston to Colon. Government forces reported approaching Colon in vessels. Prevent their landing if in your judgment this would precipitate a conflict.
>
> Acknowledgment required.[15]

Disputes flourished between Colombia and Panama over control of the Isthmus of Panama, and in the latter country revolts broke out in November 1903. No blood was shed, for Colombian troops were prevented from crossing the isthmus by the commander of the American gunboat standing nearby. Within four days there were seven more United States warships in Panama waters, and two weeks later the United States formally recognized Panama as a legitimate nation.

Historians, particularly some of those writing after World War I, picked up the allegation that Roosevelt himself had instigated the Panamanian revolution solely for the purpose of capturing control of the isthmus for the U.S. Definite answers have not been found, and authorities writing in the *Encyclopedia Britannica* summarize their account of the complex episode by asserting, "No evidence has been produced to give the allegation the slightest support."[16]

In 1904–1905 TR's reputation as an international statesman was given a greater boost by his intervention in bringing about peace between Russia and Japan. The Nobel Prize Committee, recognizing his role in ending that

Russo–Japanese War, conferred upon him its highest award for promoting international peace.

Theodore Roosevelt retired from the presidency in March 1909 and gave endorsement to his successor William Howard Taft. The next month, TR with his son Kermit sailed for Africa to begin a year-long hunting and scientific expedition. Upon the conclusion of those adventures, he journeyed to Europe, where he gave highly acclaimed speeches to listeners in Paris, Berlin, and London.

By 1910 a serious split had developed between conservative and progressive elements in the Republican Party. President Taft's positions on issues dividing the partisans caused TR to believe that his successor, rather than carrying out policies TR thought had been left in place, had aligned himself with opposing factions.

Upon his return from Europe to the United States, Roosevelt was given tumultuous receptions. He told reporters that he intended to retire, but politics was ingrained and he could not stay away from its frays. He continued to write essays for the *Outlook*, advancing his fight for what he termed "new nationalism." To him, "new nationalism" meant control by the people of political organizations and commitments insuring equal opportunities for all citizens. Essentially growing out of conservative theories, the "new nationalism" espoused by Roosevelt advocated recall of elective officers by public vote, the direct primary, and the referendum which aimed to make legislatures more responsive to popular will. Particularly the recall of judicial decisions sent shivers up spines of Republican conservatives, yet it was from this position that in 1912, TR "threw his hat in the ring."

Republican delegates met in Chicago for their nominating convention at the beginning of June 1912, and after bitter debates President Taft was re-nominated for a second term. Two months later, two thousand men and women from forty states in the Union gathered in Chicago to form the Progressive Party. The assemblage consisted of Republican leaders who were sick of their boss-ridden party. Also present were successful industrialists seeking to rebut Roosevelt's scathing indictments of the "malefactors of great wealth." Social workers who had labored in the slums of the great cities and knew the wretched lot of the poor attended, along with a miscellany of reformers and cranks bringing proposals and schemes to daunt the hardiest. Nobody was turned away. "There was room on that platform," said a young worker later, "for anyone who had seen Peter Pan and believed in fairies."

By acclamation the delegates chose Theodore Roosevelt as their preferred candidate with Senator Hiram Johnson of California as his running mate. America's first Progressive Party was launched, and two months later its champion Theodore Roosevelt, addressing enraptured followers, shouted, "We stand at Armageddon, and we battle for the Lord." Conventioneers arose to sing "Onward, Christian Soldiers," and other stirring melodies. When their adored leader declared, "I am feeling like a bull moose," the dissidents gained a symbol to stand beside the traditional Republican elephant and the Democratic donkey.

The Progressive Party Platform offered plums to everybody. It advocated the direct primary vote, the popular election of U.S. senators, and a shorter ballot. Reform measures endorsed were the initiative, referendum, recall, and easy amendments to the U.S. Constitution. Going further, the drafters pointed out that such amendments most certainly would include equal suffrage for men and women, anti-lobbying legislation, and the recall of judicial decisions. In an appeal for the labor vote, Progressives promised anti-injunction laws and trials by jury in cases of contempt arising out of injunction suits. Child labor would be prohibited; a minimum wage would be set for women workers, and there would be great improvement in systems of workmen's compensation. Moreover, a Department of Labor would be established in the President's Cabinet. There was a pledge to enact social insurance laws to protect workers against unemployment, sickness, and old age. No group was overlooked.

In their convention, which met in Baltimore, Democrats chose Woodrow Wilson as their candidate. The convention set off spirited campaigns which saw four candidates vying for the nation's top office: William Howard Taft, Woodrow Wilson, Theodore Roosevelt, and the Socialist entrant Eugene V. Debs.

Both Wilson and Taft concentrated their artillery on Roosevelt, who at the height of the campaign was shot by a maniac in Milwaukee. Wounded slightly, TR insisted on getting into the car, being driven to the hall, and delivering his prepared address. Only after all that had been accomplished would he consent to be taken to a hospital.

In that fall's election, Democrats prevailed over the divided Republicans, and the final tally showed 6,203,097 popular votes for Wilson, 4,119,507 for Roosevelt, 3,484,956 for Taft, and 901,873 for Debs. Electoral votes were even more decisive: 435 for Wilson, Roosevelt 88, and Taft 8.

For Theodore Roosevelt the results were not unexpected, and he returned to writing critical essays in the weekly periodical *Outlook*. Still very vigorous and as restless as ever, in autumn 1913, he went to South America to deliver a series of lectures, and he also agreed to lead an exploration into the jungles of Brazil to find out more about an almost unknown river shown on existing maps as the River of Doubt.[17]

The explorers fought their way for more than 1,000 miles through jungles teeming with mosquitoes and insects of every description, incredible temperatures, shortages of food, and treacherous waters. The trek was enough to kill ordinary men, and did indeed claim the lives of two of Roosevelt's safari. He himself fell ill several times but kept going. The Brazilian government, thoroughly pleased with findings reported by the intrepid group, named the river, *Rio Roosevelt*.

In March, 1914, TR was back in New York and at work assembling memorabilia as well as beginning to pen his memoirs. World War I broke out in Europe, and when America entered the conflict in 1917, Roosevelt wanted to form a volunteer division of "outdoor men" — a collection similar to his famed Rough Riders. President Wilson turned down the offer, and TR in disappointment went on the lecture circuit, speaking in behalf of Liberty Loan drives, the Red Cross, and other war related agencies.

Fevers and malaria he had contracted in Brazil kept returning to plague him, yet despite his illnesses he made numerous speeches. His grit and perseverance impressed everyone, friend or foe.

It was said that George Washington founded the nation and that Abraham Lincoln saved it. No one could deny that Theodore Roosevelt invigorated America and gave it new meanings. With his own moral character and indestructible determination, the renegade, the traitor to his caste, a leader who never ceased in his castigation of the malefactors of great wealth, he carved a niche for himself in the country's history. Theodore Roosevelt died in his sleep on January 6, 1919.

Chronology of Theodore Roosevelt, Jr.

Born October 27, 1858 in New York City

Parents: Theodore Roosevelt, Sr. and Martha (Mittie) Bulloch Roosevelt

Siblings: Anna (Bamie), Elliott, and Corinne (Conie)

Asthmatic attacks 1861–1881.

Tutored at home 1858–1874

Family Tour of Europe 1869–1870

Second Tour of Europe, this time including Africa 1872–1873

Harvard University 1876–1880 (*magna cum laude*)

Married Alice Hathaway Lee, October 27, 1880

With wife Alice toured Europe 1881

Elected to New York State Assembly 1881

Published *Naval War of 1812* in May, 1882

Bought land in Dakota Territory 1883

Wife Alice Lee died Feb. 14, 1884; Mittie (TR's mother) died same day

Signed contract to build home at Sagamore Hill, 1884

Cowboy in North Dakota Territory 1884–1885

Pursued and captured three thieves 1886

Defeated in Campaign for Mayor of New York City 1886

Married childhood sweetheart Edith Carow in London Dec. 2, 1886

Founded Boone & Crockett Club 1888

Published *The Winning of the West* 1888–1889

U.S. Civil Service Commissioner 1889–1895

Police Commissioner New York City 1895–1897

Asst. Secretary of the Navy 1897–1898

Organized Roosevelt's "Rough Riders," 1898

Governor of New York 1899–1900

Vice President of the U.S. March 4, 1901–March 8, 1901

Succeeded to U.S. Presidency upon death of McKinley, Sept. 14, 1901–1909

Issued Corollary to Monroe Doctrine, Dec. 2, 1904

Awarded Nobel Peace Prize 1906

Writer, Big Game Hunter, Political Leader 1909–1912

Nominated as "Bull Moose" candidate for U.S. Presidency 1912

Victim of attempted assassination October, 1912

Led exploring party to South America 1913

Literary Pursuits 1916–1919

Died January 6, 1919 at Oyster Bay, N.Y.

CHAPTER 3. EUGENE DEBS: REBEL WITH CAUSE

In the presidential election of 1920, nearly a million U.S. citizens voted for a man imprisoned in the federal penitentiary at Atlanta, Georgia!

Eugene Victor Debs' life began in Terre Haute, Indiana, when passions throughout the entire countryside were nearing the boiling point — a point soon to be reached in a disastrous civil conflict.

In 1851, Terre Haute had less than six thousand persons and was a raw, new area with more saloons and whorehouses than schools and churches. Men wore boots, carried guns, and spat tobacco juice, but due to its location at the intersection of the Wabash River, the Erie Canal, and the National Road hardly a mile east, the town was growing rapidly.

Jean Daniel Debs had immigrated from France two years earlier, and after six months in America he was able to persuade his French sweetheart, Marguerite Marie Bettrich, to join him. Married within the week of her arrival, the couple moved first to Cincinnati, living there for two years before settling in Terre Haute.

In the bustling community, Daniel tried several jobs before hiring with a crew laying ties for the Vandalia Railroad, the first of its kind to come through the town. Unfortunately his health broke and he was unable to continue the usual fourteen hours of hard labor. However, his wife Marguerite, whom he and everyone else called Daisy, saved the family. She invested the last forty dollars of their meager savings in a stock of groceries and opened a store in the front room of their home. Daniel thought the venture would fail, but he had learned enough about butchering that he could handle that part of the business. Within a few months, Daisy and he were earning a decent living.[1]

On November 5, 1855, in the two-story frame house with its store in front, the couple's first son was born. Daniel, still impressed by the writings of his compatriots Eugene Sue and Victor Hugo, named the newborn Eugene Victor Debs.

Five years later the Civil War broke out, and the Mississippi River was blockaded by Union troops. As a result of this stoppage, railroad centers like Terre Haute grew even faster. For a boy under ten years old, it was an exciting time. Gene Debs watched troop trains arrive and depart, although uniforms and soldiers didn't interest him as much as the giant locomotive which pulled its string of cars through the town. Railroad men clad in denim overalls swaggered through city streets, and Gene along with other boys his age ran around yelling, "Toot! Toot!" while moving their arms as if pulling a whistle. At night they dreamt about a day when they themselves would be working on the railroad.

Terre Haute had a public school which young Gene attended for two years before his father, having lost faith in it, transferred him to the Old Seminary School, a private institution. The lad wanted to learn and had a fantastic memory, but he became bored with endless repetitions in reading, writing, and arithmetic. He preferred the lessons his father as tutor gave him at home.

Gene grew up on the fringes of the Civil War, heard its talk and saw its marching soldiers going off and coming back. His happy childhood was traceable to his mother, for between him and her was a most tender relationship that lasted well into his adult life. The man so often accused of seeking to destroy the American home believed with all his heart that "man may make the nation but woman does more — she makes the home."

Gene's father Daniel was son of a prosperous mill owner in France. Daniel had received a classical education, and to his son he liked to read and discuss passages from Voltaire, Racine, Goethe or Schiller, and his favorite, Victor Hugo. Thus from his father, Gene Debs absorbed ideals espoused by democratic Europeans.

At the age of fifteen, Gene finished grammar school and was a husky lad approaching his adult height which would reach 6 ft. 1 in. He persuaded his dad it was time for him to drop out of school and get a job. His first one was painting signs for the railroad yards in Terre Haute. After a year of that work, he climbed aboard a switch engine as a regular crew member and began firing over the road from Terre Haute to Indianapolis. He was sixteen years old; his wages went up to $1.25 a night, but two years later along came a depression and he was out of a job. He was able, however, to get a lesser paying one as billing clerk, and from that position he joined the local firemen's brotherhood — the Brotherhood of Locomotive Firemen (BLF). The membership of this local was so small that newcomer Gene was elected its secretary.

About this time, he began to regret his lack of formal schooling, so he set up a program of self education. He read widely and organized a weekly discussion group called the Occidental Literary Club. Under his urging, the group started to sponsor lectures by prominent men and women.

One of the earliest guests was the orator and acknowledged agnostic Robert Ingersoll, with his attacks upon religious dogma. Another time, the club invited America's premier agitator, Wendell Phillips, aging but still vigorous enough to flay the giant monopolies. Debs wanted to invite Susan B. Anthony, who shockingly advocated votes for women, but other club members voted him down. Debs wouldn't drop the project but rented a hall himself, met the speaker at the train station, and escorted her to her hotel. As they walked together down the street, they were greeted with hostile glances and jeers from the townspeople. He later would write that it wouldn't have taken much "egging on" for the citizens to drive Miss Anthony out of the community.[2]

The faltering national economy during the 1870s gave dissidents motive for forming new parties, and one with swelling ranks was the Greenback Labor Party, a name adopted when the adherents met in a national convention held in Toledo, Ohio. In that same year, Eugene Debs gave his first political speech, championing the cause of the poor, the oppressed, and the Democratic Party. Party leaders wanted to nominate him for a congressional race. He declined their offer but did agree to run for city clerk the next year. In this contest, the entire Democratic slate was swept into office, and Debs won by 1100 votes.

In his position as city clerk, Gene's circle widened beyond railroad men. He became acquainted with business men, politicians, salesmen, and other office workers. Everyone he met liked him; he was always smiling, telling jokes, or draping his lanky figure over a bar while listening to yarns from men who traveled a dozen states.

In this environment he met James Whitcomb Riley, the Hoosier Poet from neighboring Greenfield, Indiana. Riley, six years older than Debs and well on his way toward becoming a chronic alcoholic, was a convivial companion and would become one of Debs' lifelong friends and admirers. Riley would praise Debs in at least two of his homespun verses, the best known one being:

> And there's "Gene Debs" a man 'at stands
>
> And jest holds out his two hands
>
> As warm a heart as ever beat
>
> Betwixt here and jedgment seat![3]

Debs was no teetotaler, and whenever Riley came to town the two of them would tour saloons enjoying back slapping, swapping yarns, and swilling whisky. Debs liked Riley's corny poetry and could throw in quips from his own repertoire — some of which were mawkish doggerel. Both men thought nothing of demeaning Negroes and often imitated their dialect.

During daylight hours, Debs was at his office as city clerk, but nearly every night he worked at his duties with the BLF. He served the organization for two years as assistant editor of its official journal, *The Magazine*, before being promoted to editor-in-chief. Along with that promotion, the BLF moved its headquarters to Terre Haute, and from there Debs sent out letters galore to members or prospective ones — railroad men at all levels — engineers, station masters, and day laborers with the dirt of a lifetime ground under their fingernails. Each letter would begin with "Dear Brother" and end with "Fraternally yours." It was from such camaraderie that he learned of workers' complaints: low wages, unsafe working conditions, wrecks, and innumerable hardships suffered by widows and orphans.

Slowly, membership in the BLF began to rise and along with the rise came a reputation for Eugene Debs as an energetic and fearless leader. Meanwhile, he grew more concerned over the welfare of railroad workers. Most of the companies used unsafe equipment in order to cut costs; worn rails broke under their loads; defective boilers exploded, setting fire to the wooden coaches behind them; and most dangerous of all, poor couplings caused workers to be caught and smashed between the cars.

Gene's mother pleaded with him to get out of railroading, but she admitted, "Gene listens to me. And then goes his own way."

Debs with his good looks and steady job was an eligible bachelor attractive to women in Terre Haute. Although sociable, he paid no particular attention to them; with girls he was polite and cordial but never more than that. On nights when he was not visiting the bars, he was at home writing for *The Magazine*. Very often Kate Metzel would be there, too, visiting his mother.

Kate was twenty-five, no stranger to poverty and endless housework. Her mother had died when Kate was a child, and her father married a widow with four children. Kate was given the routine of daily housework, caring for the younger children, and washing and ironing dozens of shirts for her stepbrothers.

Debs' sister Marie Heinl and Kate met and became close friends. Kate started coming to the Debs' home and met Gene and his mother Daisy there. Daisy took a liking to Kate, who came ever more frequently, visiting with Daisy while Gene worked in another room in the house. It would be late before Kate was ready to go home, and the ever chivalrous Gene, concerned about the safety of a lone woman on the streets of Terre Haute, would escort her. The escorts turned into a courtship, albeit a strange one. Rather than an engagement ring, Gene gave Kate a bound volume of *The Magazine*.

He was a slow suitor, and their courtship dragged on for three years. On June 9, 1885, they married at St. Stephens Church in Terre Haute, and the newlyweds went east on a luxurious, spendthrift honeymoon that used up all of Gene's savings — about a thousand dollars — but Gene was always profligate with his own money. When he asked his bride if she had enjoyed their eastern sojourn, Kate gave him an enthusiastic "Yes," and he responded, "That's good. For now, we're broke."

Kate would read some of her husband's writings and listen to his arguments for improving the lot of workers, but she didn't travel with him or go to hear his speeches. While Gene was extremely gregarious, she took little interest in social life, yet she was an invaluable wife. For years, she was his assistant helping with his voluminous correspondence, filing those letters as well as articles from newspapers, magazines, journals, and government documents so they would be accessible for his speeches and writings.

One of Debs' sympathetic biographers summarized Kate's contribution:

Few women have sacrificed their own interests to their husband's work and ideals as did Kate Debs. Whenever the labor movement or the Socialist Party claimed him for national tours or separate engagements she yielded cheerfully to their calls, always with the feeling that the world had more claim upon him than herself.[4]

Kate tolerated but wasn't always happy about every person Gene brought home. Most indeed were needy workers, but others included just plain vagrants, drunks, minor crooks, and once in a while a woman down on her luck. Kate liked James Whitcomb Riley and his homespun humor but came to dread visits by the Hoosier poet because they usually meant her husband would accompany him on a spree. Debs himself seldom got drunk enough to attract notice; he relished being with people and the conviviality he found in bars refreshed his unlimited energy.

As a newly married man, financial concerns were not foremost in Gene's mind. There was a budding revolt in the Firemen's Brotherhood, for as unemployment rates rose, labor conditions worsened, and in resentment workers retaliated. Members in the Brotherhood were not unaware of a Labor Council which was on its way to becoming a national union — a union which would evolve into the American Federation of Labor. Under the aggressive leadership of Samuel Gompers, this burgeoning organization was pushing hard for an eight-hour working day in all industries.

Encouraged by Debs, railroad Brotherhoods had endorsed a no-strike policy, but Gompers and his followers were getting results with militancy and work stoppages. For a time, Debs was able to keep the BLF aloof from the more radical philosophy of Gompers and his cohorts. On numerous occasions Debs championed a spirit of compromise and fair play, believing those attributes could settle all labor difficulties. It was not to be.

The fall of 1884 swept Democrat Grover Cleveland into the presidency for the first of his two non-consecutive terms, and in that year Eugene Debs agreed to run on the Democratic ticket to be an Indiana state representative. Voters in his district liked him for several reasons: his reputation for honesty and fearlessness was well-known; he could talk on equal terms with anybody; and he was common-place enough to wander around his neighborhood dressed in overalls and a railroad cap.

Ordinary laborers flocked to his support, and banners reading "Debs — Our Choice" appeared on coat lapels, bib overalls, and homespun shirts. During the frenzied weeks of August, September, and October, he traveled the district and with his tall figure, comforting voice, and long forefinger pointing toward listeners, he harangued the crowds. Voters believed him and sent him to Indianapolis to speak for them.

When sworn in as member of the State Legislature, Debs already had drafted a bill which would require railroad companies to compensate employees for injuries suffered while on duty. His bill got through the House of Representatives, but the Senate stalled it before modifying the bill so much that Debs himself withdrew it from further consideration.

He next bolted the Democratic Party which had propelled him into office and joined Republicans in submitting a bill to abolish all distinctions of race or color in the laws of Indiana; the bill lost by three votes. Undaunted, Debs joined with other liberals to offer a bill to extend suffrage to women; again he was on the losing side.

Debs felt he had failed the electorate, and when the legislature adjourned in March, he returned to Terre Haute, where he told his brother Theodore, who had run the office and edited *The Magazine*, "I'll never run for political office again."

The economy continued its downslide, and in 1887 both the Pennsylvania and the Baltimore and Ohio railroads posted notices of wage cuts. Railroad workers quickly went on strike. In West Virginia, Maryland, and Pennsylvania groups of workers blocked the tracks to keep scabs from coming in to operate the trains. State militia were called into action by the governors and as the strike worsened, President Rutherford Hayes sent in federal troops. The revolt spread to Pittsburgh, and throughout Pennsylvania enraged mobs burned shops and destroyed locomotives as well as more than five hundred freight cars. Local militia refused to fire on the strikers, but soldiers from Philadelphia killed twenty-six persons. Before the strike ended, more than a hundred workers were slain and several hundred others wounded.[5]

As the final decade of the nineteenth century opened, labor unionism was gaining force. The Knights of Labor, one of the earlier forerunners, had been split by factions and was falling to pieces while the American Federation of Labor (AFL) founded in 1881 was growing rapidly in membership as well as political clout.

Ranks in the AFL swelled even though it was founded on the principle of craft unionism, evincing almost no interest in the unskilled or more humble members of the laboring population. The Federation was made up of job-conscious workers who fought stubbornly to have their skills recognized and be rewarded by better pay and a shorter working day. Furthermore, they regarded the strike as their chief weapon.

Meanwhile like a glacier a depression spread across the country. Factories laid off workers or shut down; families were evicted from their homes, and city streets were clogged with homeless, ragged, barefoot men. In the work space where he wrote *The Magazine*, Debs, surrounded by government papers, labor journals, letters, and his own notebooks, began forming a plan for an organization which would include all railway workers — not just those in special crafts.

In June of 1893, disgruntled railway workers met in Chicago, and there Debs had an opportunity to launch his brain storm. There were wrangles, quarrels, and compromises before the plan was accepted in its final form with Debs as its unchallenged leader. On the evening of June 20, 1893, he put out a press release announcing formation of the American Railway Union.

Membership in the new organization was open to all *white* workers who served a railroad in any way except managerial employees. (The American Railway Union never rescinded its great error — the ban against Negroes.) Track crews and even coal miners and draymen were eligible if they worked for a railroad. Dues were cheap — a dollar initiation fee and a dollar a year thereafter to the national union. The Railway Union (ARU) pledged itself to protect pay scales and lengths of work days, to publish a daily newspaper, a monthly magazine, and to provide cheap insurance.

Entrance of the ARU was a sensational development in the history of labor struggles, but six days after its formation was announced, another event captured headlines. Surviving but imprisoned members of the Haymarket Riot were pardoned by John Peter Altgeld, who had become governor of Illinois. Altgeld gave as the reason for his pardons not mercy or benevolence but a miscarriage of justice that had sent them to jail. Altgeld's biting criticisms of the legal proceedings in that trial aroused passions of hundreds of citizens, and the public press stirred emotions higher by calling the governor an anarchist, socialist, and even a criminal. Similar treatment was given to Eugene Debs when in *The Magazine* he praised Altgeld's pardon message.

Debs had been able to keep the BLF away from endorsing strikes and militancy as was practiced by Gompers and the AFL, but Debs's writings in *The Magazine* and his reiteration in speeches that there was no inherent conflict between labor and capitalists didn't arouse the fervor it once did. In late 1885, *The Magazine* had carried an alarming message about the use of dynamite in labor disputes:

> Legitimate warfare in the future is to be in the interest of the weak, the oppressed, those who aspire to be free. Dynamite is to be a potent weapon in the contest.[6]

A half-year after this announcement came the Haymarket affair in Chicago. On May Day, 1886, more than forty thousand workmen put down their tools and walked off the job. Owners reacted quickly and brought in scabs as replacements. Citizens throughout the city waited to see what would happen.

They didn't have long to wait, for three days later police killed a striker at the McCormick Reaper Works. Other strikers egged on by anarchists called for a meeting at Haymarket Square to protest the killing. The assemblage was peaceful until a patrol wagon approached the crowd, and a bomb was thrown into its ranks. In the ensuing riot, seven policemen were killed or fatally wounded.

Known anarchists and labor leaders in the city were indicted for the bombing; only two of the unionists had been present at the bombing. However, the judge presiding over their trial departed from traditional practices and declared that even if absent from the scene of the crime, past utterances of the accused were incitements toward violence; hence, they must be judged guilty.

There was a flood of public protest against the judge's ruling, but Debs in his speeches and in *The Magazine* kept out of it. He was in a dilemma; protests from him would most certainly call attention to his unfortunate statement about the use of dynamite with resultant damage to the entire membership of the BLF; yet he was an unrelenting advocate of free speech and in complete sympathy with the men judged so unfairly.

Debs remained silent until after higher courts had denied all appeals by the convicted men. When he could stand it no longer, he wrote a stirring rebuttal in *The Magazine* as well as declaring on numerous platforms that the judge's ruling was a flagrant violation of the principle of free speech.

In *The Magazine* and in speeches he warned that the judge's verdict, if left to stand, would abolish free speech, making that cherished principle as dead in America as it was in Russia. His fervent assaults marked a change in the mail that poured in. Townspeople who knew Gene personally praised him, but following his indictment of an American court proceeding much of his mail grew vicious; the tenor running along such lines as: "Debs, you are a liar, thief, bandit, or murderer. You're not fit for American citizenship and ought to be deported. Beware! You'll wake up in Hell!" The letters would be anonymous and signed often *An American*.

Despite the hate mail, membership in the ARU grew; at the end of 1893, charters had been issued to eighty-seven lodges, and the organization could boast it had about 150,000 members, enabling it to put four employees on its national payroll.

A challenge to the ARU came early in the next year when the Great Northern Railroad declared a wage cut for all its workers. Debs and top assistants in the ARU were capable enough to deal with top business and industrial executives, but at the local level raw recruits were no match for the experienced and adroit negotiators the Great Northern chose. Against the advice of Debs and his national compatriots, at the local level, hat and banner-waving recruits voted to strike. Several federal judges already had issued injunctions forbidding workers to strike, and Debs along with companions at the national level of the ARU also were against such stoppages. At the local level, however, the raw recruits held sway. They voted strike, and Debs hurried to their support.

Through his pressures and persuasions, three federal judges, including the one who had issued the injunction forbidding workers to strike at the Great Northern, took hearings on both the wage cuts and the injunction. These hearings vindicated the union's positions; former pay scales were restored, the injunction was nullified, and it was affirmed that the union had an undeniable right to combine in order to raise wages.

From the standpoint of effectiveness, no previous strike in American history had ever been so successful, and it established Eugene Debs as a national leader. He wrote his reaction to the praise given him:

> The greatest tribute that was ever paid me was that of the section men after the Great Northern Strike. As my train pulled out of St. Paul, those men with shovels in hand and with happiness fairly radiating from their faces — yet with tears in their eyes — those section men stood at attention. That tribute to me was more precious than all the banquets in the world.[7]

The outcome of the Great Northern strike delighted ARU members, but it also solidified resistance by railroad magnates. More strikes were on the horizon, and one would be more gigantic and for Eugene Debs more consequential.

George M. Pullman, a cabinet maker in Chicago, had started on his road to wealth by converting old railroad coaches to accommodate long distance travelers, and in 1864, when Eugene Debs was about nine years old, Pullman built his first modern sleeping car. Gaining a large income from the invention, he founded the Pullman Car Company and established the town of Pullman on the outskirts of Chicago where Pullman workers could live. The community was no paradise, for Pullman was its only employer and landlord; the town was a feudal manor, with George M. Pullman its absolute monarch. Times were tough, and the workers, having no money to move elsewhere in search of better jobs, were forced to submit or starve.

In the spring of 1894, a majority of Pullman workers joined the American Railway Union. Dissatisfied members voted to strike, and on May 11, three thousand workers left their jobs in the Pullman shops. Three hundred men tried to remain, but they were laid off immediately because Pullman thought they belonged to the obstreperous union.

At the outset of the strike, Debs in Terre Haute knew almost nothing about it. There is considerable evidence that he did not want his new union to get into the strike. He had been told of hardships suffered by residents of Pullman, but calling the strike was an act done by Chicago brotherhoods and was neither known nor approved by the ARU. Nevertheless, the strikers were members of his union, and as soon as he learned of the stoppage, he hastened to Chicago to help them.

Even though he had tried to avoid the strike, once into it Debs took control. Newspaper reporters wrote of the "Debs Rebellion." The *Chicago Tribune* led the assault, and one of its captions read: "*Six Days Shalt Thou Labor — Bible. Not Unless I Say So — Debs!*"[8]

The strike was amazingly effective. At first, under Debs' insistence, strikers refused to work on trains pulling Pullman cars but did allow those carrying U.S. mail to go through. Corporate owners, by this time resolved to destroy the pestiferous ARU, stiffened and linked Pullman cars with mail trains, insisting they had to do so under previous contracts.

The strikers had everything to lose by violence and knew it, but railroad owners with guidance from their lawyers and Attorney-General Richard Olney brought in professional strikebreakers recruited from labor spies, racketeers, petty gangsters — the flotsam and jetsam of the city. Along with others more upstanding, these thugs were deputized; Governor Waite of Colorado called them "deputized desperadoes."

The disorder spread and crossed the state line just outside Chicago to Hammond, Indiana, where more than a thousand workers and sympathizers amassed to stop a train and force switchmen to detach all its Pullman cars. Emotions rose higher; the head of the Switchmen's Union warned that any member of his lodge supporting the strike would be subject to expulsion, and the Conductors' Union attacked the boycott in the public press.

Still there was little violence — until the Federal Government stepped in. This intervention came despite protests from Illinois Governor Altgeld, supporting sentiments from executives in neighboring states, and the mayor of Chicago.

For newspapers, the strike was a bonanza — field day, picnic, parade, and revival meeting — all rolled into one. Most newspapers including prestigious ones in the East lambasted the strikers as did the *Tribune* in Chicago. Other newspapers there were split; two, the *Daily News* and the *Record*, remained neutral; the *Dispatch*, the *Mail*, and the *Times* defended the strikers. Never before in U.S. history had there been such a mammoth work stoppage;

at its worst, more than a hundred thousand workers were off their jobs. Flush with victory in the Great Northern strike, Debs believed the strike could be settled peacefully. However, he had overlooked one huge factor: intervention by the federal government.

On the second day of July, 1894, a federal judge issued an injunction — a legal writ forbidding workers to strike. The breadth of this injunction was almost unbelievable, for under an interpretation of the Sherman Antitrust of 1890 it prohibited strike leaders from any measures, statements, or writings which might aid or contribute to a later boycott.

Under pressures from his attorney general and railroad owners, President Grover Cleveland previously had alerted federal troops stationed at Fort Sheridan, Illinois, to stand by. On July 3, 1894, without requests from state or city executives, President Cleveland ordered the entire command to go to Chicago.

The sight of armed soldiers camped on the lakefront of the Windy City provided the spark that touched off violence. Debs had not objected when state or local police were called in, for he realized they were there to prevent possible destruction of property or civic disturbance, but he was incensed by federal troops because their presence was interpreted as rebellion against the government.

There was a series of frantic meetings between Debs and municipal authorities, but when they tried to invite George Pullman to join such discussions, they were told the magnate couldn't be located. Actually, he had taken his family east to their mansion in New Jersey.

A popular humorist pictured as a shrewd Irish saloon keeper, Finley Peter Dunne, satirized Pullman's disappearance:

> This here Pullman makes th' sleepin' ca-ars an' th' constitootion looks after Pullman. He have a good time iv it. He don't need to look after himsilf. . . He owns towns an' min. . . . Whin he has throuble ivry wan on earth excipt thim that rides in smokin' ca-ars whin they rides at all — r-runs to fight f'r him. He calls out George Wash'nton an' Abraham Lincoln n' Ginral Miles an' Mike Brennan an' ivry human that requires limons an' ice an' thin he puts on his at an' lams away. 'Gintlemen,' says he, 'I must be off,' says he. 'Go an' kill each ther.' he says. 'Fight it out.' he says. 'Defind the constitootion,' he says. 'Me own s not of the best,' he says,' an' I think I'll help it by spindin' the summer,' he says piously, 'on th' shores iv th' Atlantic Ocean.' [9]

When railroad managers refused to meet with state or municipal authorities to discuss arbitration, Debs was convinced the real purpose of the railroad managers was to destroy the labor union.

On July 5th, a freight train was halted, a signal house torched, and the soldiers fired into the crowd injuring several people. The arson, bloodshed, and increasing provocations by deputized hoodlums as well as soldiers created greater problems for Debs. He kept imploring the workers to be orderly and law-abiding, reiterating that their cause was just and that the great mass of citizenry was with them.

By this time, the strike in Chicago had captured the nation's headlines. Most presses made it seem like the entire city was being despoiled. The *Washington Post* declared: "Fired by the Mob — Chicago at the Mercy of the Incendiary's Torch!" [10]

Though not as great as described, violence indeed was growing in Chicago. On July 7th, two separate troops of militia were provoked into shooting into crowds of rioters who had taunted and stoned them. Four rioters were killed and forty wounded, including some women.

During these hectic goings-on, the ARU did not hold a single secret meeting. Instead, Debs and subordinate leaders spoke to members on public highways, close to railroad yards, or in districts near the workers' neighborhoods — always begging listeners to act lawfully and return peaceably to their homes.

When two men were killed at a related disturbance in Spring Valley, Illinois, more federal troops were sent to Chicago, bringing the total there to 1936 soldiers. On July 10th, a Federal grand jury accepted an indictment against Debs and the ARU. As a result of this indictment, he and three lieutenant leaders were arrested for conspiracy to interfere with interstate commerce.

The end of the strike was in sight. Merchants on Chicago's State Street were so hostile to the ARU that they refused to advertise in the *Chicago Times* or any other newspaper which supported the strikers. The Chicago Building Trades Council called off its sympathetic strike and other unions followed suit.

The ARU's boycott collapsed quickly, leaving it the biggest news story of the year. Fourteen thousand law enforcement officers had been summoned to duty during the outbreaks; yet thirty persons had been killed and twice as many wounded. Although sympathy strikes broke out elsewhere, the center was Chicago. In that city alone thirteen were killed and fifty-three seriously injured. More than seven hundred men had been arrested, and estimates of damage ranged upwards of eighty million dollars.

Debs' initial arrest for conspiracy to interfere with interstate commerce was set aside by another arrest on a contempt of court charge for violating an injunction issued by a federal court. He and seven other ARU leaders were sentenced to jail. Debs was given the longest sentence: six months.

When the eight men were taken to jail at Woodstock, Illinois, they were permitted to bring books with them. The sheriff was agreeable, and the convicts soon turned corridors to their cells into a prison library for social sciences.

Mail to Eugene Debs, now a national celebrity in jail, was so heavy that the ARU was forced to hire a secretary for him. The eight prisoners were given special privileges, excused from usual work assignments, allowed un-limited mail, and permitted to have many visitors. Among the latter came most leaders of American Socialists.

History would indicate that Debs began serving this jail term as a waver-ing capitalist and that during his six-month imprisonment at Woodstock he converted to socialism. In truth, his full-fledged accepted of that credo was more gradual.

When the jail term ended and Debs was returned by train to Chicago, more than 100,000 persons jammed Michigan Avenue to welcome him. Quite a reception for a jail convict being released!

The Pullman strike helped establish Eugene Debs as the foremost spokesman for labor. His personal prestige continued to grow, but the strike doomed his American Railroad Union. Listeners still turned out to hear him lecture, but they were afraid to join his union. Moreover, the union's debt of thirty thousand dollars for legal and attorney fees alongside immense printing bills forced its bankruptcy. Railroad after railroad blacklisted ARU members; men were driven from their jobs and hounded from city to city.

After the collapse of the ARU, Debs kept up with demands for speeches throughout the country, continuing to meet with labor dissidents, address-ing Chautauqua societies or other reform groups. He still preached the ben-efits of industrial unionism, but interspersed with appeals for that cause, he gave more attention to the roots of discontent — living conditions for the unemployed, child labor, cruelties practiced in prisons, and the deprivation of civil rights, including denial of voting by women.

From such strenuous efforts he fell ill in the latter months of 1897 and returned to Terre Haute to recuperate. By the third month of 1898 he was on the road again, talking about socialism and selling subscriptions for Party organs such as *The Social Democrat Herald*, Victor Berger's Milwaukee *Voraerts* and Julius Wayland's *Appeal to Reason*.[11]

In 1900 Debs was nominated for the first time as the Socialist candidate for the U.S. Presidency. In his campaign, he spent most of his time trying to explain socialism — that its doctrines did not propose public ownership of white shirts and toothbrushes, but only the capital goods of the country: i. e. factories, railroads, and banks.

When ballots were counted in November, Debs had polled only 96,000 votes. He would run for the U.S. presidency four more times on the Socialist ticket. In 1904 his popular vote increased to 402,283; in 1908 it fell only slightly but gained to 420,793 in the election four years later.[12]

In the 1908 election, he took his campaign on the road, traveling coast to coast in his "Red Special" train which consisted of a locomotive with a coach, sleeper, and a baggage car packed with campaign literature. He spoke to more than 500,000 people on his journey, many of whom contributed hard-earned cash to bolster his chances. Despite his best efforts and crowd enthusiasm, his vote total in that November was only about 18,000 more than it had been four years earlier.

The reform platforms of Bull Moose Theodore Roosevelt and the New Freedoms championed by Woodrow Wilson in 1912 hurt Debs; nevertheless, his public persona bolstered his popular vote total to 900,672. On his fifth try — 1920 — he garnered his largest number of popular votes.

The overriding issue in the 1916 election was the war in Europe, which had erupted two years previously. President Woodrow Wilson was swept into office for a second term largely on the premise of having kept America out of the conflict. Gene Debs had declined nomination for the presidency but had agreed to run for a congressional seat and spoke out fervently for pacifism.

For two years, the U.S. teetered on entering the European war. Debs' speeches became ever more explicit and vehement against any kind of American involvement. In June 1918, addressing a throng in Canton, Ohio, he abhorred the ongoing havoc and insisted that the U.S. must not allow itself to be dragged into it.

Federal authorities were quick to react. He was arrested in Cleveland before the month was out and charged with violating the Espionage Act. In the ensuing trial, prosecuting attorneys argued that in his Canton speech, Debs was trying to discourage enlistment in the armed forces and promoting insubordination within its ranks.

Speaking in his own defense, Debs admitted making the talk but denied allegations of the prosecutors. Going further, he launched into arguments against the validity of the Espionage Act itself, claiming it repudiated the rights of free speech.

In two hours of testimony before the jury, Debs had this to say about the Canton speech and his beliefs:

In what I had to say there my purpose was to have the people understand something about the social system in which we live and to prepare them to change this system by perfectly peaceable and orderly means into what I, as a socialist, conceive to be a real democracy. . . .

I am doing what little I can, and have been for many years, to bring about a change that shall do away with the rule of the great body of the people by a relatively small class and establish in this country an industrial and social democracy. . . .

I would no more teach children military training than I would teach them arson, robbery, or assassination.[13]

A jury found Debs guilty as charged, and in the September that followed, a federal judge sentenced him to ten years in prison. An appeal to the U.S. Supreme Court failed, and Debs first was taken to a state jail in West Virginia before being transported to the federal prison in Atlanta, Georgia, where he was to serve the balance of his sentence.

When the 1920 election rolled around, Debs was prisoner numbered #9653 in the Atlanta Federal Penitentiary but Socialist loyalists could not be deterred; they nominated their leader for the presidency again.

There had been drama in all of Debs' campaigns but none as spectacular as the one waged in 1920. While behind bars, he polled nearly a million popular votes! An astonishing accomplishment and undeniable testimony as to the respect in which he was held by so many.

Among the plaudits sent him was a moving one from the dauntless deaf and blind Helen Keller:

I write because my heart cries out and will not be still. I want you to know I should be proud if the Supreme Court convicted me of abhorring war, and doing all within my power to oppose it. . .

You dear comrade! I have long loved you because you are an apostle of brotherhood and freedom. I have thought of you as a dauntless explorer going toward the dawn. . . I have followed your footsteps. . . and now reach out my hand to clutch yours through prison bars.[14]

There was a concerted effort to get Debs as well as other political prisoners released, but President Wilson, the liberal, refused to free the 64-year-old distinguished leader. It remained for Wilson's successor, the Republican, Warren G. Harding, to do so.

When Debs was released he was asked to go directly to the White House, and there he had a twenty-minute interview with the President. After that session he boarded a train and returned to Terre Haute where a mammoth crowd and four separate bands welcomed him home.

The life of Gene Debs did not end with his release from the Atlanta prison. He kept up a heavy schedule of speaking and wrote innumerable articles arguing the case for socialism. His health, impaired by forty-five years of indefatigable strain worsened, and he spent five years in and out of hospitals or tuberculosis sanitariums.

Only in this winter of his life was he confronted with the realities of Socialism as practiced by Soviet Russia. During most of his years as a Socialist, Debs had praised the democratic ideals behind the rise of Communism in Russia, but he had not dealt with the harsh practical realities of the world's first real-life national experiment with it.

An outspoken pacifist, Eugene Debs would have been appalled by the cruelties ordered by Nikolai Lenin and his heir Josef Stalin. Debs died in 1926, well before Stalin's grisly purges of the 1930s. In his old age Debs was just beginning to suspect that Communism as practiced there was not the Utopia he had envisioned. Stories of the atrocities had begun to filter into the U.S., but it was not until Nikita Khrushchev delivered his so-called "secret speech" in February 1956, thirty years after Eugene Debs had passed from the scene and was beneath the sod in Terre Haute, that the world learned of the horrors and scope of those Russian purges — families destroyed, men and women slain by firing squads, and thousands sent to frigid deaths while slaving in Siberian gulags. The punishments were inflicted on such charges as "treason," or "traitor to the government," or the airy "enemy of the state." Debs would have recoiled with disgust and shame over such travesties; after all, had he not been convicted on similar allegations?

In 1924, he was sixty-nine years old and still believed that a system of Socialism as his mind had formed it during his stay in the Woodstock jail would be a real solution to ills he had raved about for more than three decades. True, the belief had weakened when he heard tales of the ruthless authoritarianism in Communist Russia. A man who acquaintances said was so tender he "wouldn't kill a fly" found it hard to believe reports of the punishments and slaughter taking place there.

Several factors worked to separate Debs from the Communists. In the aftermath of World War I there had been schisms and struggles for control of the Communist Party, and the winning faction decided to split from those insisting on world-wide acceptance of Socialist doctrines and to side with the Bolsheviks who were concerned primarily with government inside Russian boundaries. In doing so, the winners were renouncing a basic tenet of Socialist Doctrine, namely, its insistence that the system must be for all nations. Debs could not agree with a departure from the very core of Socialism.

There was even a more overwhelming factor which would keep him from endorsing Communism. Debs was bone and fiber American and thoroughly Midwestern. His sensitivity to the ideas, concerns, and needs of working men and farmers was almost uncanny, and this sensitivity was missing among the leaders of Communist Russia. Many members of the Communist Party had been miners or were from towns overrun with immigrants who were there in search of work; they had little commonality. If they did elect leaders or spokesmen, those chosen were sure to be marked for repression or deportation. Authority of the state was a Damoclean sword over the heads of ordinary Communists, and Eugene Debs by nature rebelled against decrees by authorities.

His faith in Socialism as a system for the good of humans everywhere never wavered, but he would not tolerate injustices or abuses of authority.

When Eugene Debs died in 1926, tributes poured in — from the small and the great — famous writers like Edgar Lee Masters, Sinclair Lewis, Eugene Field, and from wealthy attorneys, big businessmen and ordinary day laborers. Many admired him not merely for his crusade for industrial unionism but for his pioneer work favoring women's suffrage, his appeals for social security legislation, prison reforms, and for extension of civil liberties. Most of the goals for which he fought are accepted today as rights or entitlements.

The noted author of *USA*, John Dos Passos, gave a good description of what happened after Debs was freed from prison:

> And they brought him back to die in Terre Haute
>
> To sit on a rocker with a cigar in his mouth,
>
> Beside him American Beauty roses his wife had fixed in a bowl;
>
> And the people of Terre Haute and the people of Indiana
>
> And the people of the Middlewest were fond of him
>
> And afraid of him and thought of him as a kindly old uncle,
>
> Who loved them and wanted to be with them
>
> And to have him give them candy.
>
> But they were afraid of him as if he had contracted a social disease
>
> Syphilis or leprosy, and thought it was too bad,
>
> But on account of the flag and prosperity,
>
> And making the world safe for democracy,
>
> They were afraid to be with him or to think much about him
>
> For fear they might believe him . . .[15]

For hadn't he lettered on the wall of his prison cell his lifetime creed?

While there is a lower class I am in it!

While there is a criminal element I am of it!

While there is a soul in prison I am not free!

Chronology of Eugene V. Debs

Eugene Victor Debs born November 5, 1855, Terre Haute, Indiana

Parents: Jean Daniel Debs and Marguerite Marie (née Bettrich) Debs

Education: Grammar School: 1861–1866

First Jobs: Vandalia Railroad: painting signs and then switchman

Joined Labor Brotherhood (Vigo Lodge) in Terre Haute: 1874

Marriage: June 9, 1885. Terre Haute. Indiana

The Magazine: Editor, 1880–1896

Indiana House of Representatives: 1885 (Democratic Party)

Great Northern Strike: January–March, 1894

Pullman Strike: 1894

Illinois State Imprisonment: 1895

First Run for Presidency: 1900

Other Presidential Runs: 1904, 1908, 1912, and 1920

Federal Imprisonment: 1920–1921

Death: 1926

CHAPTER 4. ROBERT M. LA FOLLETTE: UNYIELDING REFORMER

Southwestern Wisconsin is a land with streams, thinly covered rocks, and soil that makes farming less lucrative there than in other areas of the state. The land supports a variety of citizens. Irish immigrants began coming to the area in the 1830s because of the potato blight in their homeland; then came Cornish miners drawn by rich fields of lead. Later, British, German, Norwegian, or Swiss settlers trickled in. Three years before Wisconsin was admitted to the Union as a free state, it was reported that a quarter-million acres of farmland had been sold to incoming Germans.

In 1840, twenty-three-old Mary Fergeson living in central Indiana married Alexander Buchanan, Two years later Buchanan was killed at a neighborhood barn-raising, and his wife was left a widowed mother with a baby less than a year old. In Kentucky, Josiah La Follette discovered that a pretty girl he had known casually, before she married another swain, was a widow in nearby Indiana. Vowing to friends that he meant to marry her, Josiah went to Indiana, resumed the relationship with Mary, and the couple married in 1845, remaining to farm in the Hoosier State for three years.

Josiah had three brothers who were able to save enough funds to purchase more than 800 acres in southern Wisconsin. The brothers sent glowing invitations to Josiah to bring his wife and children to farm one of the plots. Thus, Josiah and Mary together with daughter Ellen Buchanan and two recently added infant brothers, William and Marion, arrived in a covered buggy and with two covered wagons to settle in Wisconsin.

On June 14, 1855, another son, Robert Marion La Follette, entered this world. His birthplace was near the tiny community known as Primrose Township, where by this time his parents had established themselves as successful farmers and community leaders.[1] The area already was a mosaic of differing ethnic cultures, and Robert grew up among them.

Bob La Follette was only eight months old when his father died, and again his mother was a widow, but this time with three children rather than one to care for.* Mary La Follette and her children were bequeathed one of the best farms in the county, and her brothers-in-law pitched in enough so that she was able to stay on the Wisconsin farm.

Details about La Follette's childhood are sketchy, and he himself gave varying versions. His autobiography begins with events when he was twenty-five years old and leaves the impression that as a youth he had taken responsibility for raising the family. Bob's mother was a strong believer in the value of an education and told friends and family members that her children were going to get a good education even if it meant reducing her income or selling part of the farm. The record will show that she had to do neither.

In 1859 when he was four years old, Bob began his formal schooling near Primrose. When possible, Mary would send her children to a private school rather than to the overcrowded one-room public school.

At that time, the state of Wisconsin had a school year officially set at three months; in 1866 the school year would be expanded to five. Young La Follette was described as "irrepressible," "extroverted," and "mischievous," yet a reasonably good student.

In the local school, he sometimes was asked to stand on the teacher's desk when reciting so that classmates could see him. He had a flair for public speaking and drama, often entertaining friends, family, and public audiences with his acting or oratorical skills. His small stature marked resemblance more to his mother than to his father, and early in life he chose a pompadour hair style to give the illusion of greater height. That pompadour would become Bob La Follette's trademark.

Bob's widowed mother was in her early forties, alone but for her children when John Saxton began courting her. Saxton, merchant, postmaster, hotel manager, and town chairman of a neighboring village, appeared to be a fine choice as stepfather for Mary's children. She and Saxton were married in 1862 and as was common practice, the wife surrendered all her authority, financial, and familial powers to her husband.

The rosier future Mary had expected failed to emerge, and Saxton, rather than being a financial mainstay, proved to be a drain. In the year of their marriage, his real estate holdings were appraised at nearly $1,000; three years later they had shrunk to less than $100. It was evident to neighbors that Saxton and his family were living beyond their means.[2]

Nor did Mary's two sons get along well with their stepfather. The rift was wide enough that Mary sent her eldest son to live with his uncle in Indiana. With his brother away from the family, Bobby La Follette became the victim of the stepfather's frequent whippings, who followed the dictum that sparing the rod would spoil the child.

The Civil War ended in April, 1865 and President Lincoln was assassinated a few days later; both events captured ten-year-old Bob La Follette's imagination. He heard news of the assassination from a neighbor and ran home to tell it to his mother. He didn't question or doubt the zealots around him who claimed the Republican Party, not the Union Army, was responsible for winning the war; that party's actions in postwar years only deepened his belief.

For John Saxton, life on the farm was not as enticing as he had envisioned and he moved the family to Fayette, a town nearby where he started another store. The children were enrolled in a private school, maintaining their position in the elite class of the community. Saxton's store, however, proved to be a failing venture, and his difficulties continued to mount. He decided living in town was too expensive, so he and Mary moved back to the farm. Bob, then thirteen, was permitted to stay in Argyle where the school was better than the one in Primrose Township. He stayed there picking up whatever jobs a teenager could find, but just before his sixteenth birthday he went back to the farm to join his mother and stepfather.

Conditions there had changed dramatically. Bob's brother William had returned to Primrose with a new wife and had taken over control of the farm. Moreover, John Saxton was old, enfeebled, and no longer able to physically abuse or even dominate sturdy sixteen-year-old Bob.

Most of his years between sixteen and twenty Bob spent working on the Primrose farm, but he found time to make frequent trips to Madison, twenty-four miles away. His stepfather died in 1872, and a year after that La Follette and his mother decided to leave the farm and move to Madison where he could attend the university.

His mother sold eighty acres of the farm and took in boarders at Madison, while Bob spent two years taking preparatory courses to make up for his educational deficiencies. At the university, he paid for part of his education by selling books and teaching in a one-room school. He also became publisher and editor of a student newspaper during his last three years of college and in that enterprise hired other students at low wages. By canvassing local merchants for advertising, he was able to earn roughly $700 for each of those three years.[3]

In college La Follette was more interested in social and extra-curricular activities than in regular academic studies. He enjoyed acting and speaking, including all phases of debate and oratory, winning an interstate competition in the latter field. In 1879, half the Wisconsin faculty voted not to approve his graduation, but the university president intervened, and La Follette received his bachelor's degree in that year.

In social matters, he began dating Belle Case, a classmate five years younger than he. Belle was a better student than Bob and would go on to obtain her own law degree — the first woman graduate of the University of Wisconsin Law School. Before that happened though, the attraction between Bob and Belle had deepened; they wanted to marry but realized they would need an income. They postponed their wedding hopes, and Belle taught school while Bob prepared to become a lawyer. For two years, the couple could see one another only when their busy schedules permitted. Belle was teaching five days per week and Bob was taking courses at the law school, reading law books, discussing legal principles with a lawyer friend, and watching trials in Madison's courts. This training was enough to enable him to pass the bar exam and be admitted to practice in February, 1880.

After their long engagement ended, the two were married on New Year's Eve, 1881, in the Case home in Baraboo, Wisconsin. The ceremony was attended only by the two families and a Unitarian minister, who honored the bride's request that the customary word "obey" be deleted from the marriage rites.[4]

Bob decided the best way to start his career as a lawyer was to become district attorney for Dane County, Wisconsin. It was a low-paying job that usually attracted neophyte lawyers, and when La Follette got the job, he vigorously prosecuted tramps, drunkards, vagrants, and other public nuisances. The job also helped him get a foot in the door to state politics.

In his four years as a district attorney, La Follette came to realize that big business leaders had captured control of the Republican Party. At the end of the Civil War, veterans streamed back into Wisconsin and resumed their places in its ethnic conclaves. Old rivalries resurfaced and new ones arose as the state actively recruited immigrants to meet labor needs in the expanding lumbering, manufacturing, and agricultural enterprises.

During the post Civil War period, the lumber industry in Wisconsin was second only to farming. Little if any thought was given to forest conservation The federal government was quick to grant sales of native pine lands to lumber companies, and as a result, lumber and railroad corporate leaders combined to dominate the state legislature as well as its congressional seats.

The boss of Republican stalwarts in Wisconsin when La Follette first ran for district attorney was Elisha Keyes, who was irritated because La Follette had failed to seek his approval. In the 1870s Wisconsin farmers were hit hard by falling prices and exorbitant shipping costs, and Keyes lost favor among the state's biggest corporate leaders due to his weak responses to various protest movements that arose among the disgruntled farmers. One of the most important bigwigs directing lumbering as well as railroad management was Philetus Sawyer, who seized political control from the faltering Keyes. La Follette as a beginning district attorney, and perhaps dramatizing his role, viewed Sawyer as his opponent and himself as "a man eager to win out over adversity by doing what is right."[5]

The official record of La Follette's performance as district attorney and his own account do not match well. His boast of a record number of convictions is not fully substantiated. He did set a record in the lower municipal court with eighty-six convictions of various public nuisances during his first year, but these convictions were for minor transgressions such as disorderly conduct. He lost his cases prosecuting murderers, extortionists, and adulterers. Nevertheless, he gained public attention and popularity, and when he ran for a second term he received 118 more votes than his Democratic opponent.

Elisha Keyes was ousted as postmaster in Madison and kingmaker for Republican Party and was replaced by George E. Bryant. Bryant, a well-known and wealthy cattle breeder, had been a Civil War general, a state senator, and a county judge. He was, in fact, the judge who had prevented John Saxton from making further sales of the La Follette farm.

La Follette had built an adoring vision of his own father, and he seemed to find in Bryant the attributes he had imagined his father had possessed. La Follette considered Bryant a great moral teacher, a wise gentleman, a good lawyer, and a fine judge.[6] Bryant in turn thought highly of La Follette and urged him to seek higher political office. Bryant suggested that La Follette run for the U.S. Congress; in essence, Bryant became the godfather in Robert La Follette's political career.

La Follette declared himself a candidate for the U.S. Congress in late spring of 1884 and had just begun his campaigning when he fell ill — a behavior pattern that would show itself frequently throughout his adult life. When he was involved in a campaign, an intensifying tangle with railroad magnates, or a prolonged congressional fight, he gave it all his effort, working long hours, sleeping little, and neglecting a proper diet.

While La Follette lay in his sick bed at home, Bryant and other supporters conducted his first run for Congress. Their efforts and La Follette's popularity with rank and file citizens won him victory by a slim margin, 491 votes, and he went to Washington in the following March to take a seat — at age thirty the youngest member of the Forty-ninth Congress. Within the House of Representatives, the new congressman made many friends, among them "Czar" Thomas B. Reed from Maine.

Throughout his first term, despite friendship with House leaders, La Follette authorized no major laws, introduced few bills, and let others define the issues. Keenly aware of conflicts dividing Republicans back in Wisconsin, he began building foundations that would assure his re-election in 1886 and 1888. He asked a friend in each ward and township in his district to compile lists of active Republican workers and open-minded Democrats who might campaign for him. When Republicans regained the White House in 1889, La Follette was able to secure appointments or census enumerators for such allies at home, who not only shunted off rival candidates but were ready to work for his re-election.[7]

Congressman La Follette came to an understanding with the interest groups that descended on Congress even before the opening gavel fell. Interest groups sent lobbyists to the capitol to inform legislators of how dairy farmers, railroad workers, or small bankers in their district would react to a specific bill. So sensitive was La Follette to events at home that he did not need lobbyists to tell him what was popular there. The most striking example of his perspicuity is his continued defense of the dairy industry — a mainstay in Wisconsin's economy.

During the 1880s, meat packers began manufacturing large amounts of oleomargarine to compete with butter. La Follette bitterly condemned oleo, and tried his best to get the federal government to tax it out of existence. He consistently denounced oleomargarine as a "monstrous product of greed and hypocrisy," often going further to say,

> Ingenuity, striking hands with cunning trickery, compounds a sub-stance to counterfeit an article of food. It is made to look like something it is not; to taste and smell like something it is not; to sell for something it is not, and so deceive the purchaser. It follows faithfully two rules: "Miss no opportunity to deceive," and at all times to "put money in our purse."[8]

Dairy farmers throughout Wisconsin were grateful, and other industries in the state such as wool-producers and growers of cigar-leaf tobacco were equally supportive when he pushed hard for high tariffs to protect them against foreign competitors.

La Follette by 1890 was a speaker in demand throughout Wisconsin and adjoining states because of his prominence in the U.S. Congress. In that year, too, in his run for a fourth term he touted his role in helping frame the McKinley Tariff. By doing that he won allegiance from farmers and workers in his home district who were convinced that high tariffs were their best protection.

Wisconsin had a higher proportion of immigrant voters than any other state, and ethno-religious conflicts overrode economic matters when voters went to the polls that year. Catholic, Lutheran, and other clergymen turned their parishes into branches of the Democratic party, and in the fall's election Republicans were swamped. La Follette went down in defeat, and at age thirty-five he left Washington to move back to Wisconsin and resume law practice.

Robert and Belle La Follette chose to live in Madison, where law practice was more promising than back nearer the farm homestead, and La Follette had plenty of cases. He used his undeniable talent for oratory in courtrooms and became recognized as one of the region's best jury lawyers. He relished the opportunity to win approval from common persons and when address-ing a jury he would pull out all the stops in his dramatic presentations.

Despite his record of antagonism against railroads in general, he solicited legal business from some of them, defending them against charges made by passengers or workers who alleged the railroad had acted improperly or had been very negligent. For his services La Follette received an annual retainer from the Milwaukee Railroad in addition to free passes for himself and his family. Such conduct was so contradictory that critics deemed him a charlatan ready to serve any person with money to pay. Less vehement observers viewed his actions as coming from his own deep-seated convictions: he was certain that he, possibly even he alone, could discern right from wrong in all cases, and act accordingly.[9]

Discontent among American farmers and rural residents rose rapidly within five years after the end of the Civil War. The opportunity to obtain free lands or lands at a nominal price lured thousands of settlers to move west from Eastern regions. More and more acres were plowed and sown to grow corn, wheat, or cotton. This was true not only in the Midwest and Northwest where corn and wheat were the chief products but in the Southwest where cotton and tobacco could be grown. Illinois, Iowa, Nebraska, and Kansas flooded markets with corn; Minnesota and the Dakotas produced bushels of wheat, and in Texas, where entire areas had been opened for the growing of cotton, more beef was raised than the nation's citizens would buy.

Consumption of commodities increased but not nearly as fast as did increased production. The result was that too many bushels of grain, too many bales of cotton, too many tons of hay, too many pounds of beef were thrown on the market each year. Shipping costs spiraled upwards as railroads raised rates and awarded preferred customers with rebates or lowered fees, and with surpluses available, the prices farmers received for their crops plunged. The table below indicates the plight farmers faced.

AVERAGE MARKET PRICES OF THREE CROPS 1870–1897[10]

	Wheat	Corn	Cotton
Years	(Per bushel)	(Per pound)	(Per pound
1870–1873	106.7	43.1	15,1
1874–1877	94.4	40.9	11.1
1878–1881	100.6	43.1	9.5
1882–1885	.80.2	39.8	9.1
1886–1889	.74.8	35.9	8.3
1890–1893	70.9	41.7	7.8
1894–1897	.63.3	29.7	5.8

Advancement in the means and speed of transportation during the latter half of the nineteenth century vastly expanded markets for American crops. Abundant harvests found their ways into the very centers of trade not only in the United States but throughout the world. Most farmers refused to believe their plight came from overproduction; instead they blamed railroads, brokers, and money-grabbing corporations. Railroads were the targets of dissatisfied farmers. As the frontier moved ever farther west, the length of the haul of crops increased, and railroads exacted higher fees, charging whatever the traffic would bear. Irate agrarians howled their questions: "Why should a Kansas farmer have to sell his corn for eight or ten cents a bushel when the New York broker could and did demand upwards of a dollar for it?" "Why should transporters like railroads or glib salesmen like brokers get so much more than the farmer, who working from sunrise to sunset tilling the soil and harvesting the crops, ever hope to see?"

La Follette recognized the mélange of discontent and capitalized on it in his drives for the Governorship of Wisconsin. His first run for that office was in 1896 when he canvassed friends and mailed more than a thousand letters to state politicians trying to win their endorsement in the nominating convention scheduled to be held in Milwaukee. Old guard Republicans in the state feared actions La Follette and his supporters might take if he won the office, so they raised more money and defeated his challenge.

La Follette, bitterly disappointed, started looking for other ways to promote his candidacy in 1898. When that year rolled around, he agreed to run for the Governorship again, but he left most of the actual campaigning to supporters. His platform as announced through newspapers and brochures pledged more justified taxation with every corporation doing business with the state.

The pledge was aimed particularly at railroads, which were being taxed on their incomes rather than on their physical property. Other objectives in his platform were elimination of the caucus and convention by replacing both with the nomination of candidates by Australian ballot at a primary election. Also, public officials were to be prohibited from accepting favors from railroads such as free travel passes, sleeping car accommodation, meals, and so forth. Once again, despite even greater popular support than two years previously, La Follette was defeated. He rationalized the loss by declaring,

> We had not fought wholly in vain; we had so stirred the state upon progressive issues that our opponents did not dare risk the rejection of the platform which we presented. . . .Temporary defeat often results in a more decided and lasting victory than one which is too easily achieved.[11]

A week after the defeat, La Follette took his family to California, where he could rest and recuperate. Then when he came back to Wisconsin, he doubled his efforts, touring the state, giving lectures, lambasting corporate greed, and adding to his already considerable luster. When liberals within the party encouraged him to make a third try for the Governor's chair, he at first demurred, but soon added that he was available to do whatever was necessary.

The outlook for him was rosier in 1889, for several of his critics among old guard Republicans had died. More liberal party members had joined with La Follette's faction, bringing with them money for larger campaign expenditures. In this third run, La Follette campaigned more actively than he had previously. He continued to plead for statewide primary elections, but otherwise his talks centered around national issues. He extolled the solidarity of the McKinley–Roosevelt presidential ticket, endorsed the forcible annexation of the Philippines, approved the U.S. war with Spain, and favored American expansion in the Caribbean and the Far East — all positions favored by traditional Republicans.

La Follette campaigned vigorously throughout the summer and fall of 1889. He made 208 speeches in sixty-one counties to about 200,000 people, covering 6,500 miles in the last three weeks. His efforts paid off, for on November 5, 1900, Wisconsin voters went to the polls and awarded him the largest majority of votes ever given to a gubernatorial candidate up until that time.[12]

In Madison, La Follette began his first term as governor with high resolve and eager determination. His election seemed to hold promises for several groups of voters: protection for dairy farmers from inroads being made by oleo manufacturers, giving local reformers more control of utilities, reducing patronage extended by railroads, and societal acceptance of Scandinavians His goal was to make political organizations more responsive to popular will, and he announced an agenda to do so by restricting lobbying, reducing campaign expenditures, upgrading the state's educational system, curbing monopolies, and passing laws regulating pure food, child labor, and workers' compensation.

He was more successful in campaigning than he was in achieving results as Wisconsin Governor. He announced in February that his first objectives were to secure the direct primary and to revise the tax laws. His arbitrariness in choosing these two out of all he had proposed ruffled feathers among the flock. Moreover, with Wisconsin swamped in economic turmoil he faced other handicaps. More than half the state's farms were heavily mortgaged; 80% of the population owned only 10% of the state's wealth, and 1% of the population owned half the state's property.[13]

The harmony which had marked his campaign dissolved, and party battle lines were redrawn as old antagonisms flared again. He attributed the opposition as products of machine politicians, whom he said were being led by "insidious bribers and whoremongers." He did not try to implement all his programs immediately. In his first term, he felt it would be enough if he could get enacted a comprehensive primary election law and revise taxation laws so that railroads would be taxed on actual property evaluation.

In addition to attacks upon corporate greed, he had decried the abuses of patronage whereby political hacks were given appointments irrespective of their qualifications. Therefore, voters supporting La Follette expected him to make judicious appointments based upon merit rather than subservience. But that was a goal easier to promise than to achieve. Even before sitting in the Governor's chair, he was besieged by office-seekers wanting appointment; appointments would become a *bête noire* throughout Lafollette's career — a beast he never mastered. He repeatedly promised to fill offices with his best "unbiased judgment," while also saying, "I shall not forget my friends."

Anti-La Follette forces claimed that as governor he abused patronage more than his predecessors had done. Clerks, bureaucrats, highway and factory inspectors, temporary personnel such as ticket sellers and guards, and especially game wardens — these were positions he could and did award. His skilful use of patronage helped him build a coterie of supporters variously called rebels, insurgents, reformers, progressives, populists, and sometimes the even more odious name "socialists." He insisted his selections were made on merit, but such insistence evaporated when the majority of state employees who failed the civil service examinations he himself had championed were shown to be game warden appointees.[14]

Wisconsin legislators stonewalled and failed to pass laws La Follette had promised. Chagrinned, he responded with a scolding and asserted that their dereliction was cheating and betraying the voters. In retaliation, half the Republican members in both houses of the legislature signed a manifesto criticizing Governor La Follette for encroaching upon the constitutional rights of the legislative branch. Furthermore, they formed a brigade to fight his progressive movement.

La Follette's innovative reform measures were stymied. Despite intra-party strife, his popularity with voters remained high, and he was re-nominated overwhelmingly for a second term in 1902. In a 145-page highly emotional account of his victory, he prepared a booklet entitled "Voters' Handbook," in which he restated his lofty goals and alleged they had been thwarted by corrupt methods in the legislature.[15]

He began his second term as governor by reiterating that his desired goals had been defeated by corruption and bribery. Even in his second term he was unable to win enough supporting legislation for railroad regulation — an issue that had helped propel him into office.

La Follette and like-minded supporters had become known as progressive Republicans, but they faced opposition not only from Democrats but from old-time stalwarts within their own party. La Follette's use of patronage and his years of struggle had honed him into a master politician able to weld farmers, laborers, and citizens from all walks of life into a group of solid supporters convinced that he was a leader dedicated to making their homes and lives more safe as well as trying to promote more equitable redistribution of society's wealth and power. Despite struggles within Wisconsin Republicans, fervent backers urged him to run for a third term, to continue to push for his desired legislation, and then accept the U.S. Senate seat in 1906 when the term of its present occupant, Charles Quarles, expired.

Accepting the challenge, he campaigned for the governorship vigorously throughout summer and fall, and in November, 1904, was elected by a razor thin majority, 51% of the voters. Not long after beginning his third term as governor, Wisconsin voters also approved the direct primary although the new law did not take effect until September, 1906. Nevertheless, La Follette was rightfully entitled to boast that he had helped make Wisconsin the first state in the nation to require that all candidates for public office be subject to the direct vote of the people.

There was little doubt that La Follette was considering a return to national politics, although he denied that in seeking a third term as governor he had sought pledges that would send him to the U.S. Senate. His family finances had fallen into a deplorable condition, and in efforts to make money as well as satisfying his ego, he decided to go beyond Wisconsin. A speaking tour of Eastern and Western states not only would gain him larger audiences but also would bring sizeable honoraria.

He was inaugurated as governor for the third time on January 2, 1906, and on the same date became one of its senators. In order to take the senate seat, he had to resign the governorship, which he did after appointing a long-time supporter to take his place.

As governor, La Follette had tried to restrict lobbying, advance the state's educational system, curb monopolies, regulate pure food laws, eliminate child labor, and improve workers' compensation. He was successful in getting the direct primary vote system accepted, but otherwise his accomplishments from the Governor's chair were minimal. Some were adopted after his tenure in that office was over, and more important, effects of his persuasion remained; much of the reform agenda he attempted eventually became models for other states.

By 1906, the year in which La Follette started his career in the U.S. Senate, the nation's economy had improved since the depression ten years earlier. Prosperity was not shared equally, however, for big businesses were even bigger, and trusts continued to dominate entire industries. Less than 1% of manufacturers held more than a third of the nation's capital and employed more than one-fourth of its manufacturing workers.

A majority of voters looked toward President Theodore Roosevelt for reform leadership. In office five years after his predecessor William McKinley had been assassinated, TR was using the bully pulpit to lambaste wealthy wrongdoers and malefactors for widening the gap between rich and poor. In the U.S. Senate, Republicans met in caucus to solidify party control. Loyalty to party was a cardinal virtue, and the bosses used their power — committee assignments, campaign funds, and patronage — to bring newcomers aboard.

La Follette was one of the newcomers, and party stalwarts decided to sidetrack this ambitious freshman by making sure he had no influence over important or pending legislation. He was put on insignificant committees and buried under a mass of routine senate business.

A newspaper publisher, William Randolph Hearst, not yet the mogul he was to become, gave a huge boost to insurgency claims when he ran a nine-months series entitled "Treason of the Senate." The essays charged that senators were bowing to wishes of corporations and lacked the courage of Theodore Roosevelt and the rebellious Robert La Follette. Bold language and graphic detail in the essays aroused great interest among consumers, taxpayers, and common citizens, so the coterie of senators beginning to gather around La Follette basked in ever-widening public support.[16]

Early in his senate career La Follette solidified his independence by championing the Hepburn Act, a measure aimed at regulation of railroads. President Roosevelt endorsed the Act, believing it would modify discriminating rail rates, but La Follette wanted a law that would benefit consumers and was convinced that the Hepburn Act would bring benefits only to shippers. In an impassioned speech extending over several days, he proposed an amendment empowering the Interstate Commerce Commission to set rates based on the railroads' ownership of physical property. His amendment was defeated 40 to 27, but it drew the lines for future debates.

Never one "to get along by going along," La Follette took other actions which alienated some fellow Republicans while gaining endorsement from others. He championed a bill that protected timber rights of Wisconsin's Menominee tribes from lumber companies; he charged that monopolistic ownership of coal mines always meant higher prices for consumers; he prepared and introduced a measure that would withdraw coal lands from sale until Congress could guarantee competition and lower prices, and he submitted a resolution to investigate the elevator trust.

Most of the proposals he submitted during that first session were defeated and some were postponed until the next session, but his speeches and often his arguments won praise from muckrakers and the daily press which complimented him in battling for the consumer.

After the senate adjourned in June, La Follette set out on a five-month speaking tour in the West. His purpose was twofold: to gain money needed to repay loans and to carry his message that large corporations were destroying the ethics of competition and community. The trip extracted a heavy toll upon his health but was rewarding, for the speeches drew large crowds in which jeers and hisses from opponents were drowned out by cheers for what he was saying. During those five months his speeches before civic and Chautauqua groups not only supplemented the family income but gained him national exposure as leader of reformists in the U.S. Senate.

Many of the issues which marked the Progressive Era related to the conservation of natural resources: land, water, timber, and coal. At first, President Theodore Roosevelt gave hearty approval to Senator La Follette's positions regarding coal mines, but the veneer of friendliness which both professed soon wore thin and was replaced by rivalry. Roosevelt and La Follette belonged to the same party, and TR was a great conservationist, one who strove for more efficient use of the nation's resources. He aimed to achieve that by having the government monitor and reform monopolistic practices of private owners. La Follette would go farther and would bring private owners to heel by giving government title to natural lands and then lease them for grazing or mining rights to corporations or citizens groups.

Early in 1907, soon after Congress began it second term, President Roosevelt promised to support La Follette's bill to withdraw mineral lands from corporate exploitation. Opposition mounted and Roosevelt, an executive who decided a half loaf was better than none, switched his support to a weaker bill. La Follette complained to his wife Belle that he had been betrayed.

Relations between La Follette and Roosevelt slid further downhill when the President withdrew his support of physical valuation of railroad properties by the Interstate Commerce Commission. Roosevelt was out of office in 1908 but was still a political leader to be reckoned with. His successor, William Howard Taft, was expected to follow paths marked out in the two preceding administrations, but trouble and disharmony erupted.

The financial Panic of 1907 provided a background for Rhode Island Senator Nelson Aldrich's proposal to issue $500 million in emergency currency backed by state, municipal, and railroad bonds. La Follette resisted the bill and broadened his own analysis. He charged that fewer than a hundred businessmen affiliated with investment banking houses constituted a "Money Trust" which controlled business and industrial life of the country, and he documented his case with the names of 97 members of the "Trust."

In 1909 Congress began debating revisions of tariff laws. The House submitted its revised bill first, one which called for free admittance of coal, iron ore, hides, flax, and wood pulp; there also would be reduced duties on iron, steel, lumber, chemicals, and refined sugar. A more conservative Senate ignored the House version and put together an undisguised protectionist tariff. Iron ore and flax were restored to the taxable list; increased rates were put on iron and steel imports, and agricultural products were maintained at former levels.

Led by La Follette, a group of dissident Republicans in the Senate tried to strip the tariff bill of its high pretense. Hot debates followed, and the dissidents began to be known as "Insurgents" or "Reformists." The final bill coming out of a conference committee was returned to the House where it passed 195 to 183 with 20 Republicans voting against it. The Senate passed the measure with a vote of 47 to 31 with 7 insurgent Republicans voting with the Democratic minority.[17]

Inspired by the positive press his brand of progressivism was attracting, La Follette in 1908 began weighing his chances for the presidency. Theodore Roosevelt bowing to precedents had announced he was not going to try for a third term, and although both he and La Follette shared similar goals with the reform movement, the personal animosity between them had increased. La Follette's backers proclaimed him as the logical successor to Roosevelt, and he did nothing to detract from that perception.[18] He accepted the accolades but didn't campaign openly, preferring to leave such promotion to lieutenants.

La Follette did his campaigning on the floor of the senate, where his flamboyant oratory kept adding to his reputation as a fearless progressive. He attacked the Aldrich bill to issue emergency currency backed by railroads as merely another attempt to use the federal government for corporate enrichment, and he reiterated his assertions that railroads should be taxed on the actual worth of their physical assets.

His senate oratory did not revitalize his chances to win nomination for the presidency, however. Republicans gathered in Chicago's Coliseum the third week in June, 1908, and on the first ballot nominated William Howard Taft, already endorsed by the doughty Theodore Roosevelt. Robert La Follette received twenty-five votes out of Wisconsin's total of twenty-six. In chagrin, he swallowed his pride and congratulated Taft before firing more of his own fusillades at the Money Trust.

To promote greater coverage of his ideas he decided to go beyond the senate and create a national magazine. He launched *La Follette's Weekly Magazine* in January, 1909. He was editor-in-chief, his wife Belle ran the "Home and Education" department, and his children wrote articles whenever they felt so inclined. The magazine's circulation ranged between 30,000 and 48,000 in its early years.

When it became clear that Senator Aldrich and his conservative faction of Republicans had no intention of lowering the tariff and were in fact intending to raise it, thus harming consumers even more, dissidents in the upper chamber cooperated more closely with La Follette.

He was acknowledged leader of a group of insurgents which included Jonathan Dolliver of Iowa, Moses Clapp and Knute Nelson of Minnesota, Coe Crawford of South Dakota, Elmer Burkett and Norris Brown of Nebraska, Albert Cummins of Iowa, William Borah of Idaho, Jonathan Bourne of Oregon, Albert Beveridge of Indiana, and Joseph Bristow of Kansas. The insurgent cause was so important to all of them that different ethno-religious background and customary senate jealousies were set aside as the rebels championed the interests of consumers: "poor workers and farmers" in the lexicon of Bristow, "humble homes" for Cummins, and workers eking out meager existence "at the poverty line" according to Beveridge.[19]

The insurgents' four-months battle against the Payne–Aldrich Tariff failed, and in August of 1909, the senate passed the measure 47 to 31 with La Follette, Beveridge, Bristow, Clapp, Cummins, Dolliver, and Nelson casting the only negative Republican votes.

Nevertheless, by the end of his first term in the senate, La Follette had shaken its conservative faction and divided its Republican members. Throughout the country he was recognized as leader of a swelling growth of aggressive and progressive senators and governors. In his run for a second term in the senate, he won handily amassing 78% of the final vote.

He continued to enjoy favorable press coverage and a growing national reputation, yet his relations with President Taft were even less cordial than with Roosevelt. President Taft had been diplomatic enough to seek advice on congressional matters from several prominent Republican senators, including La Follette, and had invited the Wisconsin progressive to come to the White House. La Follette, whether from pique or political plans of his own, declined and sent in writing his recommendations to President Taft for judicial appointments and on pending congressional legislation. La Follette raged to Belle when his recommendations were not followed, declaring that plots in the White House were trying to destroy him. Taft in turn told aides that La Follette habitually put out "false and misleading statements."[20]

In the first month of 1911, insurgent senators with La Follette in the forefront organized the National Progressive Republican League with announced goals: 1) election of U.S. senators by direct vote of the people, 2) direct election of delegates to national conventions, 3) amendments to state constitutions providing for Initiative, Referendum, and Recall, 4) primaries for nomination of elective officials.

La Follette wanted to bring the admired Theodore Roosevelt into the NPRL camp, but the former president was cautious. Professing to be in sympathy with the League's propositions, TR said there should be modified limitations and he warned against letting enthusiasm override reason.

Acrimony touched off by the Payne–Aldrich Tariff smoldered until 1910 when more fuel was added. A squabble within the administration led President Taft to fire his Secretary of the Interior. Republicans in the Senate promptly created an investigative committee whose majority report supported Taft's action, but the minority, chiefly insurgents, were defended by Louis Brandeis, an astute lawyer hired by *Collier's Weekly*. Rivalries rose further as muckrakers and reformers in the press took up the cause of the dissidents.

As the election year of 1912 approached, the nation's Republican Party was badly split. With high hopes, La Follette had announced his candidacy, but he was apprehensive about the intentions of the enormously popular Theodore Roosevelt. Roosevelt entered the race as a Bull Moose candidate to defeat Taft, and pressures rose for La Follette to withdraw. He answered by saying that he would stay in "until the last gavel falls at the convention."

La Follette's 1912 campaign was a strenuous one that ended disastrously. He was on the road day after day, hour after hour, giving speeches to followers throughout the country. Audiences overflowed with enthusiasm, and he responded in kind. Platform oratory, his deadliest sword, was the weapon he used. Some critics considered him a dangerous man, not only because of what he said but also because of his portentous way of uttering it. The *Saturday Evening Post* called him a poet and an artist — his own best audience: "When he speaks a stirring thought nobody is more deeply moved than he."[21]

In the late summer of 1912 when La Follette's campaign for the presidency was in full swing, he insisted on giving a scheduled speech to the Periodical Publishers Association meeting in Philadelphia. He arrived at the banquet hall around 11:00 P.M. when the more than 500 guests already had dined and listened to numerous speakers, including the Democratic candidate Woodrow Wilson.

When La Follette was presented, he opened on a hostile note by declaring that because he too often was misquoted by the mainstream press, he intended to read his prepared forty-five-minute address. The audience was immediately alienated by the prospect of listening to forty-five more minutes of oratory and by his tactlessness in demeaning fellow journalists.

In his speech that night, La Follette said that newspapers were the single most powerful means of educating the public on political issues, and then he excoriated newspapers for betraying the trust of the people. The evening and program had been organized to bring magazine and newspaper publishers together, and attacking either of them was an egregious error. Failing to realize what he was doing, La Follette rambled through his *faux pas*.

That affair in Philadelphia burst the balloon of presidential hopes for La Follette. Few new members were drawn to his camp, and even former supporters were dismayed. One newspaper summarized the debacle by declaring, "We do not want a man for President who forgets what he has said, and repeats it several times."[22]

The election of 1912 was more messy than usual. The field was crowded with candidates, and voters were not just split; they were splintered. The Republicans suffered most. Theodore Roosevelt had broken with the party and had run on an independent Bull Moose ticket. Some Roosevelt's backers had been lukewarm at the Republican convention though, saying they were for La Follette if he could get the nomination. La Follette had failed in that attempt although he had been given the gratuitous vote of all 24 of the Wisconsin delegates. Republicans Taft and Roosevelt called each other names, and their dissensions drove lots of voters to look elsewhere.

Democrat Woodrow Wilson, former college professor, president of Princeton University, and then governor of the state of New Jersey, was the chief rival. Wilson had lifted spirits of his party by advocating liberal positions known as the New Freedoms — some of which were patterned after the reform movements advocated by La Follette's insurgents or the Socialists led by Eugene Debs, Even the Socialists were divided into two groups: one led by Debs and another named the Socialist Labor Party sponsoring a candidate from Massachusetts. Beyond these factions was the Prohibition Party with Eugene Wilder Chafin of Illinois as its champion.

When the votes were tallied in November, 1912, it was clear that Democrats had won by a great margin. La Follette was returned to the senate for a second term, but otherwise it was a debacle for his party. Democrat Woodrow Wilson received less than 42% of the popular tally but won over four hundred electoral votes, and his party took more than two thirds of the seats in the House and held its own in the senate. The final count showed Wilson with 81.92% of the electoral votes, Roosevelt with 16.57%, and Taft with 1.51%.[23]

As governor of New Jersey, Woodrow Wilson had overseen passage of an impressive list of reforms — public utility regulations, workmen's compensation, food inspection, and urban corruption — measures La Follette and insurgents had been promoting for over a decade. At the outset of Wilson's presidencies, despite their identities with opposing parties, harmony prevailed between him and La Follette. La Follette approved of Wilson's rhetoric, especially after the former college professor made several complimentary statements about the Wisconsin reformist's ideals.

The election of 1912 shattered Republican unity. In contrast with the rigid party discipline of Democrats, insurgents and conservative elements within the Republican party battled each other. Campaigns had been waged on domestic issues, and references to foreign matters were hardly mentioned. Such emphasis would change with a dramatic event which occurred on June 28, 1914, at Sarajevo, capital of the province of Bosnia. There two revolver shots were fired from the gun of a young Bosnian patriot; the first bullet mortally wounded Archduke Franz Ferdinand, heir to the Austrian–Hungarian throne, and the second killed his wife.

Within two crowded weeks, Austria declared war on Serbia; Germany declared war on Russia and France. Belgium had been overrun by German armies, and Great Britain in defense of Belgian neutrality had taken up arms against Germany.

Two years later the U.S. still proclaimed neutrality, and President Wilson called upon fellow citizens to remain impartial in thought as well as in action. The war in Europe eroded the harmony between La Follette and Wilson.

La Follette's position on foreign policy had evolved slowly. He had defended the abortive 1905 revolution in Russia, and unlike most Republicans had voted for Philippine independence in 1907. Otherwise, when it came to foreign affairs, he half-heartedly had agreed with his party's positions. La Follette's reform followers had ballooned in numbers because he successfully had centered his fire on railroads and the domestic power of large corporations.

A social revolution broke out in Mexico in 1911–1912, and President Taft along with other conservative Republicans suggested that the U.S. might have to intervene in order to save American property. An infuriated La Follette charged that such intervention was being encouraged by wealthy American businessmen who wanted to protect their investments.

Wilson had succeeded Taft, and by 1914 when war in Europe broke out, Congress had passed several so-called neutrality measures which in essence had moved the U.S. closer to actual involvement. President Wilson's attitude toward Germany hardened. He called for military preparedness in the U.S., and he also allowed American investment bankers to lend billions of dollars to the Allies in order to buy U.S. goods, thus creating more jobs for workers and markets for farmers.

La Follette argued that Wilson's policies were not neutral but in fact were measures that would harm consumers and add profits to financiers. Senator La Follette declared that if war was the result of a trade policy that produced prosperity, then he favored peace and depression.

He was not alone in his criticisms. In 1915, Secretary of State William Jennings Bryan, the nation's foremost orator and twice defeated candidate for the presidency, resigned from office in protest of Wilson's policies, insisting they could only lead to war.

In truth, the administration's measures were designed to help the Allies, and as President Wilson became more interventionist, the insurgent senator from Wisconsin grew more intemperate. The gap between the two widened.

In 1916 La Follette introduced a bill that would establish an advisory referendum that would have to be carried out before the country could declare war. He and fellow insurgents like George Norris and Moses Clapp were joined by Democrat Bryan and his followers in working feverishly to get the measure approved. The administration blocked their move for such a referendum, and in consequence a coalescence of senators voted it down.

In 1917, Germany stepped up its submarine warfare, and American shippers refused to send cargoes into the Atlantic unless the government provided armed protection. In February of that year, President Wilson asked Congress for authority to arm merchant ships. By the time his request reached the Senate floor, less than 49 hours remained before the session was scheduled to adjourn. La Follette quickly organized a filibuster that would give voters time to restrain the rush toward war involvement, but Wilsonians learning of his intentions had circulated a petition signed by 97 senators demanding an end to the filibuster.

When La Follette arrived to deliver his speech, he found his name had been omitted from the list of speakers. Nevertheless, he rose to speak, but a quick senate vote of 52 to 12 forced him to sit down. Although he had been denied the privilege of speaking against the bill to arm merchant ships, he and his cohorts had succeeded in preventing its passage.

The *Cincinnati Press* asserted that *"Von La Follette"* took his orders from the Kaiser. An angry President Wilson led the torrent of abuse that fell upon La Follette and his fellow dissidents. Wilson told the press,

> A little group of willful men, representing no opinion but their own, have rendered the Great Government of the United States helpless and contemptible.[24]

A month later, President Wilson, despite the uproar and dissent in congress and country, issued an executive order permitting owners to arm their merchant ships and enter war zones. Nine days later German U-boats sank three American vessels.

Neutrality had been a long, rocky road for Wilson. For more than three years he had refused to be stampeded by either war hawks in his cabinet or by La Follette, Norris, and their coterie of critics. He had been re-elected on the slogan, "He kept us out of war," and he hoped for a "peace without victory" in which the U.S. as the chief neutral would be able to help shape a just and lasting peace through establishment of a League of Nations. Germany's decision to expand submarine warfare, the sinking of the British ship *Lusitania*, and the bungling German propaganda, had ended all that. The President called for a special session of the U.S. Congress to meet on April 2, 1917.

In his epoch-making address on that date, President Wilson did not begin to speak until 8:40 P.M., and delivery of his carefully drafted message — one he had prepared largely by himself and on his own typewriter — took 32 minutes. In the address, he reviewed the history of negotiations with Germany, described the deaths of innocent American citizens aboard vessels sunk by German submarines, and in general explained the failure of neutrality. There had been no alternative, and he turned to his recommendation:

> With a profound sense of the solemn and even tragical [sic] character step I am taking. . . I advise that the Congress declare the recent course of the Imperial German Government to be in fact nothing less than war against the government and people of the United States; and it {the U.S.} formally accept the status of belligerent such has been thrust upon it, and that it take immediate steps to put the country in a more thorough state of defense and also to exert all its power and employ all its resources to bring the Government of the German Empire to terms to end the war.[25]

In the senate, La Follette predicted the body would vote ten-to-one against declaration of war if his call for a referendum were approved. His hope for a referendum ended when the Senate defeated the proposal, and two days after President Wilson delivered his war message, the upper chamber voted 82 to 6 for war. The six anti-votes cast came from Republicans La Follette, Norris, and Asle J. Gronna joined by Democrats Harry Lane, William Stone, and James K. Vardaman.

La Follette had endorsed most of Wilson's domestic policies, but from the very beginning of the war in Europe he opposed taking sides in the conflict, insisting that cooperation with any one of the belligerents would be endorsement of violations of international law and the "shameful methods of warfare." Persisting in criticisms, he railed against the President's measures to finance the war, and he led opposition to the military draft and the Espionage Act. Throughout 1917 and 1918, by claiming repeatedly that the U.S. had no business in the war and had been drawn into it by lies and trickery, La Follette became one of the most hated men in the country.

In August, 1917, he introduced a War Aims resolution that called on the U.S. to declare its strategic goals, to condemn continuation of the war for purposes of territorial annexation, and to demand that the Allies restate their peace terms immediately. His call was rejected and only fueled more public anger against him.

The next month, he addressed members of the Nonpartisan League's convention in St. Paul. The crowd's enthusiasm that night encouraged him to put aside his prepared text and speak extemporaneously. He admitted that the U.S. had legitimate grievances against Germany and technical rights for most of its actions. Then he alleged that four days before the British ship *Lusitania* sailed, Secretary of State Bryan had warned President Wilson that the vessel was carrying explosives and six million rounds of ammunition. In words which drew thunderous applause, La Follette shouted, "the comparatively small privilege of the right of an American citizen to ride on a munitions loaded ship flying a foreign flag is too small to involve this government in the loss of millions and millions of lives."

A jingoistic press gave varying reports of La Follette's address that night, but most all of them were written to leave readers with the belief that he was a traitor mouthing unpatriotic lies and distortions. Secretary of State Bryan denied having any knowledge of munitions aboard the *Lusitania* prior to its sinking, with the result that La Follette's address raised more rancor against him than any of his previous speeches. The fervor rose even more when former President Theodore Roosevelt urged La Follette's expulsion from the Senate, calling him a liar — "a sinister enemy of democracy, a 'Shadow Hun,' and the most dangerous political leader of the analogue to the Bolshevik agitation."[26]

La Follette was not silenced, and his continued opposition to the war alienated him from many citizens while welding more closely around him a few liberals and academic friends. He was particularly hurt when in January 1918, four hundred and twenty-one faculty members at the University of Wisconsin his home base signed a petition deploring "his failure to support the government in the prosecution of the war." Nevertheless, he continued to speak, whenever permitted, in the senate where he lost on most issues and won only minor victories. The end of the war did not end La Follette's criticisms. Insurgent numbers had dwindled, but he remained their indisputable leader.

While Allied victors deliberated over peace plans, a gigantic revolution broke out in Russia. In America, the Wilson administration and corporate businessmen frightened by the possibility that such infection might spread across the Atlantic moved quickly. President Wilson sent American troops into Russia where they joined British and other Allied forces already there in a *de facto* war against the Bolsheviks' revolutionary regime.

La Follette and his followers by contrast championed the Bolsheviks' cause, and in the senate he supported Hiram Johnson, his colleague from California, when that senator offered a resolution demanding withdrawal of American troops from Russia. Johnson's call failed by a single vote.

A Red Scare whipped up by press and zealous prosecutions swept America, and La Follette redoubled his efforts as watchdog of the public good. He continued to strive for revision of child labor laws, to denounce bonds by which wealth was able to escape taxes, and to cast aspersions on President Wilson for standing with the rich and currying favor with big business institutions of the country.

The Peace Conference after the end of World War I began meeting in Paris on January 12, 1919, and the fourteenth point of President Wilson's proposals called for establishment of a League of Nations which would oversee guarantees of independence and territorial integrity. La Follette spoke out against the stationing of American troops in Russia along with his castigation of the secret nature of the Peace Conference going on in Paris. His most bitter attack was against the proposed League of Nations. For *La Follette's Weekly*, he wrote,

> By ratifying this document [the proposed treaty] in its present form, we shall involve this country in the quarrels and dissensions of Europe for generations to come... and prevent the U.S. from turning its energies to the solution of its domestic problems without reference to bewildering imperialism and diplomacy... If we go into this thing, it means a great standing army; it means conscription to fight in foreign wars... a blighting curse upon the family life in every American home...[27]

The Congressional elections of 1918 were more restrained than usual. President Wilson told voters that if they approved of his leadership they ought to return a majority of Democrats to both Senate and the House of Representatives. When returns came in, it was clear that his plea had not been heeded, for Republicans captured more votes. The make-up of the Sixty-sixth Congress showed in the Senate, 49 Republicans and 47 Democrats; in the house, 239 Republicans and 194 Democrats.

In July 1920, the Covenant of the League of Nations along with the Versailles Treaty was placed before the U.S. Senate for ratification, and President Wilson declared that acceptance of the League would assure future peace. Wilson had returned from Europe exhausted and ill but had insisted on taking a trip across the country in order to present his case before the highest tribunal, "an appeal to Caesar." His speaking tour was undertaken against advice from friends and doctors; obviously his health was not up to it. On September 26, 1919, he suffered an apoplectic stroke while en route from Colorado to Kansas and had to be returned to Washington as a hospital patient (where as an invalid unable to care for himself he lay for five years until his death in 1923).

As the election of 1920 drew near, differences over foreign policy clearly divided the two major parties. Democrats aligned themselves solidly behind the League of Nations with a platform asserting that the League "ought to be ratified immediately without reservations which would impair its essential integrity."

Republicans declared that the Covenant of the League of Nations failed to promote agreements necessary among countries if the peace of the world was to be protected. Republicans promised also to bring about such agreements "without surrendering the right of American people to exercise their own judgment and power in favor of justice and peace." Controversy over the League swept the country and dominated the U.S. Senate where by constitutional authority foreign treaties had to be judged before being approved or rejected.

Democrats at their convention in the summer of 1920 chose James M. Cox of Ohio as their standard bearer, and Republicans in their gathering named Senator Warren Gamaliel Harding from the same state as their champion. The Socialist Party under the leadership of Eugene Debs was on the ballot as was the Farmer-Labor Party. La Follette would have been the prime choice of this fourth group except for the fact that he insisted his platform would have to be his own and not one prepared by labor elements.

Presidential campaigns that year were spiritless affairs; less than half the eligible voters went to the polls. Warren Harding had conducted a "front porch" campaign on the slogan "back to normalcy;" he won handily, and Republican majorities were returned to both houses of congress. Observers opined that it was not so much an endorsement of the platitudes and ambiguities of the Republican candidate as it was rejection of everything Wilson had espoused, including the League of Nations.

Without Wilson's leadership, the Treaty of Versailles and the League of Nations were doomed in the U.S. Senate. There Henry Cabot Lodge proposed a series of crippling amendments, and La Follette, too, was against the treaty as Wilson had submitted it. So in a rare alliance, the rebel bloc led by La Follette teamed with Republicans to defeat the proposals. The final tally put La Follette in company with insurgents and conservative Republicans alike, and the result was that in November, 1919, the Senate rejected the measures by a vote of 55 to 39.[28] Robert La Follette's career was far from ended. In the senate and in speaking engagements throughout the nation he kept adding to his nickname "Fighting Bob" as he continued to attack corporate misdeeds. Among his targets was a coal and oil lands bill which would lease public lands to private corporations. He formed and led a filibuster charging that such leasing would destroy the very heart of programs progressives had scratched out. His efforts in this cause were successful when the Congressional session ended in March, 1919; his speaking marathon had helped kill the bill.

In the summer of that same year, a special session of Congress passed the Susan B. Anthony constitutional amendment giving women the right to vote. In truth, La Follette was a Johnny-Come-Lately to the cause of women's suffrage; his wife Belle Case was active in that cause far longer than he. For fifty years after the Civil War, the proper goal for a woman was becoming a wife and mother. Women, particularly those from urban and middle class society, formed loose knit groups aimed to combat the growing evils of alcohol consumption. Their efforts resulted in militant attacks on the nation's saloons. Women were still denied the right to vote — a right granted to nearly all white men — and a few feminine leaders were determined to remedy the deficiency.

In the summer of 1869, Susan B. Anthony and Elizabeth Cady Stanton, two of those leading the women's suffrage movement, came to Wisconsin for a statewide rally. There they found a hotbed of temperance workers ready to shift goals from destroying saloons toward other reform measures, including winning for women the right to vote. By the time Belle Case got her law degree from the University of Wisconsin, the rhetoric of the Women's Christian Temperance Union was no longer limited to alcohol consumption.

The suffrage cause gave Bob La Follette's wife a forum to express her own views which would be endorsed by her husband. Invited to address a U.S. Senate Committee on Woman Suffrage, on April 26, 1913, Belle La Follette insisted,

Equal suffrage will make better homes... for home, society, and government are best when men and women keep together intellectually and spiritually. . . .Woman suffrage is a simple matter of "common sense" and will not bring about any great immediate changes because . . . men and women of the same family should hold somewhat similar views, much as fathers, sons, and brothers do now.[29]

La Follette sensing the tide favoring suffrage for women gradually worked the issue into his speeches. In 1912 he tried to capitalize on the longevity of his commitment to equality:

I have always believed in woman suffrage, to the same extent as man suffrage, for the reason that the interests of men and women are not superior nor antagonistic one to the other, but are mutual and inseparable. . . Woman suffrage is but an extension of the principle of democracy. . . Co-suffrage, like co-education, will react, not to the special advantage of either men or women but will result in a more enlightened better balanced citizenship and truer democracy. . . . We cannot have real democracy while one-half of the population is disenfranchised.[30]

It would be seven years before an amendment granting voting rights to women would reach the floor of the U.S. Senate. On June 4th of 1919, the Senate passed the Susan B. Anthony constitutional amendment granting women that right, and Senator Bob La Follette arose to join those standing in unanimity to applaud the measure — an action that had been more than seventy years in its making.

La Follete's health, always precarious because of stressful schedules, suffered a series of setbacks. He fell ill in the summer of 1920, and surgeons at Mayo Clinic in Rochester, Minnesota, removed his gall bladder. After a period of convalescence he turned his attention to alter the Mineral Leasing and Water Acts in order to bring about better prices for consumers. Again, he was disappointed when the Senate rejected his amendment. His tormented mind drove him into other causes. One was promotion of a graduated estate or inheritance tax; another was to oppose proposals to enlarge and strengthen the U.S. Navy. He decried the "enormous profits" made by private industries gained through government contracts for such military enterprises.

He used his persuasive skills outside the Senate, too, in *La Follette's Magazine* and on lecture platforms throughout the land. While La Follette was adding to his reputation as spokesman for consumers, party leaders in both the executive and legislative branches of government kept up their disdain. After La Follette's speech in the Senate urging the administration not to ratify the peace treaty between the U.S. and Germany, from his sick bed former President Wilson said the "guilty senators" voting against his cherished dream were among the "puny persons" standing in the way of a lasting peace.[31]

Many citizens welcomed Warren Harding's administration as a "return to normalcy" following the tensions and disputes of World War I. Harding had been in office less than three months before at the request of Albert Fall, Secretary of the Interior, he ordered transfer of control over naval oil reserves in California and Wyoming to the Secretary of the Interior.

La Follette, who had spent most of his Senate years trying to preserve those lands, was outraged. His animus toward Harding rose further when the President given opportunity to appoint Supreme Court Justices, chose four very conservative ones. La Follette began promoting a constitutional amendment that would allow Congress to override the Executive's "veto" power. His readiness to tamper with elements set forth by framers of the American Constitution alienated some fervent supporters. President Harding retaliated by saying that La Follette was jealous of all men who succeeded and that the senator was trying to support his trite charges "that graft and wealth are in control of our government."

La Follette got satisfaction when an investigation disclosed that a major oil reserve known as the Teapot Dome in Wyoming had been released to magnate Harry Sinclair's Mammoth Oil Company. The matter escalated and became the greatest scandal perpetrated during the administration of Warren Harding. Moreover, the Teapot Dome affair enhanced La Follette's reputation as a staunch defender of the public welfare and an enemy of corruption among the industrial giants.

In 1922 La Follette was reelected to the senate by Wisconsin citizens who awarded him with a whopping 278,552 votes, the largest majority ever given to a public official at that point in the state's history. He now was a recognized power in the senate where few bills could be passed without his sanction.

By 1923 his presidential aspirations had returned, and he undertook a trip to Europe where he hoped through speeches and contacts with dignitaries his stature as a statesman knowledgeable about foreign affairs would be further polished. His tour lasted three months during which he visited leaders in England, Germany, the Soviet Union, Poland, Austria, Italy, Denmark, and France.

When he traveled to Moscow, in addition to his wife Belle his party included newspaper columnist Lincoln Steffens and sculptor Jo Davidson. Belle later would write for the *La Follette Weekly* glowing articles about the system of government they found in Russia; her husband's reports were more restrained. He noted that Lenin, then in his final illness, was beloved by

the Russian citizens, but La Follette was disturbed by the lack of free elections, no free press, suppression of civil liberties, and the outrageous exile of
political opponents.

The devastation and rampant inflation he found in Germany was particularly upsetting to La Follette, and upon his return to America he introduced an unsuccessful bill in the senate to grant $10 million in relief to save
the *Deutschland* people from starvation and to help them build a democratic
government.

In the twenties he kept up his attacks on profits made by powerful corporations after receiving special privileges by the government. Signs of aging
had appeared in his public presentations; the square jaw that had been a
trademark of his fighting spirit began to sag; the pompadour mane of dark
hair had turned white, and his eyes once intense and piercing now looked
tired, and he squinted more often. Yet he remained the politician and still
yearned to be president. By the opening of 1924 he had begun to collect signatures on petitions from local supporters.

Labor unions, Socialists, and farm blocs made up the core of the Progressive Political Action group which hoped to propel a third-party candidate.
The federation swelled to include representatives from the Social Gospelers, campus groups, National Association for the Advancement of Colored
People, League of Women Voters, and other organizations. The disparate
factions focused on ousting conservative Republicans, and La Follette was
undeniably the only person with enough stature to bring any hope of victory.

The Conference for Progressive Political Action (CPPA) met in Cleveland for a nominating convention and enthusiastically endorsed him. The
convention was a noisy, youthful affair — a majority of the delegates were
under 40 — with speakers representing Socialists, farmers, newly-enfran-
chised women, the Farmer–Labor Party, and blacks. All predicted victory as
did New York Congressman Fiorello LaGuardia, who declared, "I speak for
Avenue A and 116th Street, instead of Broad and Wall Streets."

The CPPA was a motley organization, attracting former insurgents and
intellectuals From New York came an endorsement by W. E. B. DuBois,
along with authors Theodore Dreiser and Thorsten Veblen, anthropologist
Franz Boas, Socialist Norman Thomas, and birth-control advocate Margaret
Sanger. Holdovers from the 1912 struggle who came to march under La Follette's banners in 1924 included Harold Ickes, Jane Addams, Gilson Gardner,
and Amos Pinchot.

Despite the flair and enthusiasm of the CPPA, it had inherent handicaps.
The federation was plagued by a shortage of funds and many of its leaders
lacked the experience and skills necessary to schedule and run an effective

national campaign. Moreover, there were huge cultural and ethnic differences among the disparate factions.

La Follette tried to paper over the splits, but some could not be covered up and his attempts to do so aroused further ire. No issue among the Progressive of 1924 was more divisive than the racial one. Along with urbanization, the Ku Klux Klan had prospered in trying to preserve evangelical religion, enforce prohibition, and suppress blacks, Jews, and Catholics. Condemning discrimination in any form, La Follette had taken a strong stand and declared, "I am unalterably opposed to the evident purposes of the secret organization known as the Ku Klux Klan." Such forthrightness won him support from the NAACP and from influential black leaders, but drew wrath from the Imperial Wizard of the Klan, who labeled him "the arch enemy of the nation."

As election day approached, the CPPA began falling apart. Its hasty collapse drew La Follette's judgment that it disintegrated because it had been "made up of various economic and political groups whose purposes were other than progressive political action."

The November election squashed hopes of La Follette and fellow Progressives. He received 16.5% of the popular vote, John W. Davis, the Democratic contender, got 28%, and Calvin Coolidge, Republican, won first with 54%.

The presidential run in 1924 was Robert La Follette's last hurrah, for the campaign took a heavy toll on his health. He suffered a series of heart attacks in the spring of 1925 and grew increasingly dependent on nitroglycerine and pain medication.

The fourteenth of June was his birthday, and in 1925 he was seventy years old. Four days later, ill and confined to bed with his wife Belle attending him, "Fighting Bob La Follette," the rebellious non-conformist — a man who spent his life battling corporate greed and wealth — slipped the chains of earth and took his place in history's chambers.

Chronology of Robert Marion La Follette

Born . . . . June 14, 1855, Primrose, Wisconsin

Early Schooling . . . . Primrose, Wisconsin.

University of Wisconsin . . . 1875–1879

Admitted To Wisconsin Bar . . . 1880

District Atty., Dane Co., WI . . . 1880–1884

U.S. House of Representatives . . . 1885–1891

Private Law Practice 1891–1900

Governor of Wisconsin . . . 1900–1906

U.S. Senate 1906–1925

Voted Against U.S. Declaration of War . . . April, 1917

Wisconsin Efforts to Remove Him from Senate seat. . . 1917–1918

Acknowledged Leader of Insurgents 1919–1925

Opposed League of Nations 1918–1919

Ran for U.S. Presidency (Progressive Party) 1924

Died in Washington, D. C . . . . . June 18, 1925

Chapter 5. George W. Norris: Liberal Independent

The 76,653 square miles that make the State of Nebraska is an area dependent upon agriculture in one way or another. Westward from the Missouri River on its eastern edge, half the state is farm land where fertile silt lies over deep loess soil. Coronado and his men probably came through the area in 1541 to find it inhabited by Indians of the Plains, later called Pawnees.

The French attempted to claim some of the land, only to cede it to the United States through the Louisiana Purchase, and the territory was a natural high-way in the 1840s and 1850s for pioneers heading west over the California, Mormon, or Oregon Trail. Wagons loaded with household goods left deep ruts in the soft valley soil.

In 1854 and 1855 the land was involved like neighboring Kansas in fierce struggles concerning slavery in new territories, and it was in the latter year that one of Nebraska's most distinguished citizens was born. In truth, his birth occurred elsewhere, but his notable life is indubitably linked with the Cornhusker State.

The American Civil War was three months old when George William Norris, the second son of Chauncey and Mary (née Mook) Norris, was born on June 11, 1861, in York Township, Sandusky, Ohio. The rapidly growing city of Cleveland was not far away and even nearer was Sandusky Bay with one of the best harbors on Lake Erie.

Chauncey Norris died before George was four years old, and although by this time the frontier had moved well beyond Ohio, George's boyhood knew many of the characteristics of pioneer life. He was a strong and active teen-ager able to do a man's work, whether it be splitting rails, shocking wheat, or husking corn. He also found time to hunt squirrels, rabbits, and quail and became proud of his skill with .22 rifle or 12 gauge shotgun.

George's mother was determined that her children should have the best education possible. No hardship or personal sacrifice was too great if it would enhance the education of her children.

George went through the elementary years at a district school in Mt. Carmel less than a mile and a half from his home. After finishing grammar school, he and his sisters rented an apartment in Berea, Ohio, where they attended Baldwin University. Out of funds after a year at Baldwin, George took a teaching job at Whitehouse, Ohio, and from that teaching experience he saved enough money that, when supplemented by whatever he could make working for farmers in the vicinity, he could go to the Normal School at Valparaiso, Indiana.

At Valparaiso he was active in debate and related speech programs as well as in parliamentary procedures; he had been introduced to those rules at Baldwin. Twenty-two years old when his formal education educated, he made an exploratory trip to the Pacific Northwest, but the promised land there was not up to his expectations.

Five years after her first husband died, George's mother married Isaac Parker, an elderly Pennsylvanian. She and her new husband were able to pur-chase eighty acres of land in Johnson County in Nebraska, and in 1885 she gave the deed to that land to her son George. George went to Nebraska, took up residence, and was there for nearly two years before a business association with a local nurseryman earned him enough money to buy a quarter-section of land near Beaver City and open his own law office.

Norris made his first bid for public office in 1890 when he ran for prosecuting attorney of Furnas County, Nebraska. Economic conditions were bad in the Midwest then, and the Populist Party was being formed. An ardent and unabashed Republican, Norris lost that first race largely because numerous Republicans chose the Populist cause, but two years later he ran for the same office again and won. As the county attorney, he gained a reputation for being stern but fair and forthright.

Drawn inexorably into politics, his identity as a Republican was indisputable. He acknowledged his allegiance and confidence in the party.

> I was an ardent Republican. I thought the Republican party was perfect... My loyalty and zeal as a Republican never faltered in those years. . . I found myself importuned frequently to become a Populist, but I remained loyal to my Republican faith. . . I campaigned ardently for Republican nominees and spoke in schoolhouses all over the county.[1]

Living conditions were harsh throughout the Midwest with its crop failures and low farm prices. There was a single, blistering afternoon in 1893 when thousands of acres of corn were burned by a scorching wind from the south. Three years after that there was the strange paradox of bountiful crops but corn would sell for only eight or ten cents a bushel — if it could be sold at all — a price so low that many farmers burned it as fuel.

Low prices encouraged farmers to try overcoming their debts by raising more crops, which meant buying more acres. Banks and lenders were ready with mortgages at ten per cent, so lenders profited while indebtedness soared. It was estimated that in Nebraska, South Dakota, and Minnesota there was one mortgage for every three residents.[2]

Agrarian distress was manna for reformers with the result that Populists were the strongest political party in Nebraska during Norris's two years as Prosecuting Attorney for Furnas County. Populists were even stronger in 1895 when he ran for the district judgeship — a district comprised of eight counties in the extreme southwest corner of the state. Despite opposition from Populists, Democrats, and a few conservative Republicans, Norris won the office, and in later years (perhaps with senile hyperbole) he would declare that the seven years he served on the bench in Nebraska were the most satisfactory period of his life.

In 1902 he won nomination as a Republican from the Fifth Congressional District in Nebraska, and followed that win by eking out a narrow victory over Democrat and Populist rivals. When Norris arrived in Washington to take his seat, Theodore Roosevelt was in the White House, succeeding to the presidency after the assassination of William McKinley. Muckraking, the journalism of exposure and battles against corporate malfeasance, ran almost parallel with Theodore Roosevelt's two administrations.

Throughout his first congressional term, George Norris hewed to the Republican Party line and did not join the clan of insurgent liberals; on the contrary he seemed to be an admirer of Roosevelt and of Joseph G. Cannon, powerful Speaker of the House. As a freshman representative Norris believed that enlightened government was only possible through the election of Republicans and that nearly all virtues of democratic government were embodied in the Republican Party.

When Norris attended his first meeting with the committee to which he had been assigned, he was rankled when he learned that it was the Speaker of the House, not the committee preparing a bill, who determined whether the bill should be presented to the House membership.

> The senior Democratic member of the committee . . . made a motion that the chairman of the committee should seek a conference with the Speaker and ascertain whether or not we should be allowed to have a public building bill at that session. I could not understand why the Speaker should have anything more to say about it than anyone else, and especially the members of the committee.[3]

Insurgents in both House and Senate had gained strength by the time the presidency of Theodore Roosevelt came to an end. Speaker of the House Joseph Cannon, the "Iron Duke," was viewed by the rebels as an ogre thwarting the public will. Cannon had once answered a Progressive's question by saying, "The function of the federal government is to protect life, liberty, and property. When that is done, let every tub stand on its own bottom and let every citizen 'root hog or die!' "

The Speaker appointed the Rules Committee which had responsibility for deciding what matters were to be brought up in the House. Speaker Cannon appointed Rules Committee members at his whim, and thus through appointments he maintained dictatorial power to control all legislative issues to be debated.

In 1908 Representative Norris began marshaling forces to curb the Speaker's power. His opportunity came when an obscure Land Office agent accused the Interior Secretary under Roosevelt's successor, President William Howard Taft, of conduct unfitting for public office.

President Taft had appointed Richard Ballinger as his Secretary of the Interior, and at the time Gifford Pinchot, a wealthy Pennsylvanian whose influence had converted Theodore Roosevelt to natural resources conservation, was still Chief Forester in the Department of Agriculture.

Indignant when Ballinger allowed the richest coal mines in Alaska to be turned over to a private corporation, Pinchot accused Ballinger of being a traitor to Roosevelt and conservation programs inherited from him, which presumably were still in force. When Pinchot admitted he had been supplied with confidential government information and had used it in his attacks on Ballinger, President Taft demanded Pinchot's resignation. Taft, however, took no action against Ballinger for his malfeasance.

Two months after Pinchot had resigned, a coalition of resurgent Republicans and Democrats led by Congressman Norris of Nebraska overthrew Joseph Cannon's control of House debate.

In a whitewashed hearing, Secretary Ballinger was exculpated first by the Attorney General and then by Taft himself. A resolution for a joint investigation of the affair passed the Senate and was referred to the House, where it was expected that Speaker Cannon would appoint only committee members loyal to the Administration. Norris, convinced that a fair investigating committee would not be appointed by the Speaker, persuaded fellow representatives to amend the pending resolution by striking out members "appointed by the Speaker" and inserting "elected by the House."

The arguments had not been settled when a day or so later "Czar" Cannon ruled that a census bill was privileged and could be considered although not on the regular House agenda. Norris, quickly using his own parliamentary knowledge and skills, presented a resolution under which House members rather the Speaker would appoint members of the powerful Rules Committee. Ensuing debates drew speakers from Populists, Democrats, Insurgents, and Republicans — both conservative and liberal. A slightly weaker amendment was adopted before the resolution from Norris gained a majority vote made possible by cohesion of Insurgents and Democrats — a vote which ended the Speaker's total control of agenda and appointments.

For the election of 1912 the badly-split Republicans held their nominating convention in Chicago and without great enthusiasm nominated President Taft for a second term. Dissenters claiming to represent the Progressive Party marched off to hold a rump session of their own only a few blocks away. There, before members cheering with evangelical fervor, Theodore Roosevelt, Rough Rider Colonel, in a fiery speech, eyes narrowed and teeth snapping, gave his heart to them and promised to run for president if Progressives would confirm him in a regular convention.

A month later the Progressive Party, formed only a year and a half earlier, met in the same Coliseum that had seen Republicans nominate Taft.

In contrast with the Republican gathering, the Progressive Convention was an enthusiastic, noisy assemblage, more rally than convention. Slated to be Theodore Roosevelt's running mate, square-faced Senator Hiram Johnson from California led his state's delegates into the hall as he carried a banner proclaiming:

> I want to be a Bull Moose
>
> And with the Bull Moose stand,
>
> With antlers on my forehead
>
> And a big stick in my hand.[4]

Bull Moosers drew support from small businessmen, farmers, professors, social workers, and high-thinkers as well as from women like Jane Addams and from wealthy backers who felt that "standing at Armageddon," as their champion Colonel TR put it, would not be too perilous for the nation's business structure.

Because of earlier achievements and the added drama of having been victim of an attempted assassination, Theodore Roosevelt, leading the Bull Moose faction dominated headlines. Although still a nominal Republican and that party's legal nominee for the Senate, George Norris broke ranks to support TR and join the Bull Moosers because he could no longer accept the complacent leadership of President Taft.

The November election revealed the breach between insurgents and regulars within the GOP. Insurgents swept the Midwest and West: Wisconsin, Michigan and Indiana, and all of the states west of the Mississippi except for four mountain ones. Taft carried only two states, Utah and Vermont. Roosevelt won in Pennsylvania, Michigan, Minnesota, South Dakota, California, and Washington. Woodrow Wilson swept the rest, winning 435 of the 531 electoral votes. In the popular vote, he was a minority finisher, garnering 6,300,000 to 4,100,000 votes for Roosevelt and 3,500,000 for Taft.

As elsewhere the Republican Party in Nebraska was rent with factionalism. Popular election of senators under the Seventeenth Amendment would not become effective until May 31, 1913, but Norris, running as a Progressive Republican, defeated a regular party rival for the state's senatorial nomination. Disruption in the GOP gave Democrats control of the presidency and of Congress, but on January 22, 1913, the Nebraska legislature in accordance with the mandate of the state's voters elected George Norris its senator, and he returned to Washington to begin his career in the nation's upper chamber.

Initially George Norris was in favor of most of the New Freedoms espoused by incoming President Woodrow Wilson. Like Wilson, Norris believed that the farmer and the laborer were entitled to a fair return for their toil. When the returns were not forthcoming, it was because of greed within giant trusts, railroads, manufacturers, middlemen, and Wall Street financiers. As a liberal, Norris argued that help be given to the average American, and he wanted to use government in achieving that end. He shared with Wm. Jennings Bryan, the Great Commoner, a conviction that agriculture was fundamental to the well-being of Americans and that average citizens if not deprived of their just rights possessed enough intelligence and judgment to make democratic government function successfully.

During his first term in the senate, Norris battled to amend the Underwood Tariff, urged a graduated income tax, proposed a conservation measure and led calls for several congressional investigations, including one for judging Attorney General James McReynolds' fitness for appointment to the Supreme Court.

Norris, Bryan, Theodore Roosevelt, Wilson, and La Follette were all progressives in the sense that each had a common desire to help the average American, and each was ready to use the federal government to achieve that end. They differed in methods, however. Roosevelt with his patrician background was motivated by *noblesse oblige*, Wilson by scholarly and didactic principles, Bryan by agrarian and religious dogma. Norris was more akin to Robert La Follette than to the other progressives.

La Follette was six years older than Norris, and both had known the discomforts and miseries of poverty in their boyhoods. Both struggled through college under severe financial strains; both had grown up believing in the virtues of the frontier: equality, individualism, and the common man. The two held differing views about the value of political parties, however. Both began their careers as Republicans, but La Follette quickly bucked the local machine and fought against the two major parties, Norris remained identified as a Republican for more than half a century.

The Democratic platform which in 1912 helped usher Woodrow Wilson into the White House promised a variety of measures: lower tariff, enforcement of antitrust laws, a federal income tax, states' rights, direct election of senators, a single presidential term, utility regulation, banking reforms, and recognition of independence for the Philippines. Many of President Wilson's "New Freedoms," therefore, won approval from Senator Norris. It was foreign policy that spoiled the harmony.

The war that erupted in Europe in 1914 drew attention away from domestic problems, and Senator Norris along with other reformists agreed with President Wilson when he urged American citizens "to be impartial in thought as well as in action" concerning a "war with which we have nothing to do, whose causes cannot touch us." Actions by the American Administration and by private corporations soon belied such lofty sentiments.

Prior to 1917 the U.S. tried to remain isolated politically from the European belligerents, but the nation was profiting immensely from the conflict. American trade with Allied Powers boomed and far outstripped any commerce with the Central Powers. Furthermore, huge loans made to Allied countries, particularly France, undermined Wilson's claims of strict neutrality.

Germany announced its submarine blockade of the British Isles in the middle of February, 1915, stating that it would target even neutral ships. Norris endorsed Secretary of State Bryan's attempt to dampen the flames by urging President Wilson to prohibit Americans from traveling on belligerent ships entering the war zone.

For nearly two years conditions in the Atlantic grew steadily worse, and President Wilson's neutral stance fell apart. At the beginning of February, 1917, he announced the breaking of diplomatic relations with Germany, and later in that same month he asked Congress for authority to arm merchant ships, enabling them to fire upon attackers in order "to safeguard the rights of peoples at peace."

The Sixty-fourth Congress then in session was scheduled to adjourn on March 4th, and La Follette with help from Norris and others opposed to steps which in their judgment would drag America into war organized a filibuster in order to delay putting President Wilson's request for a vote. Anti-German feeling had soared even higher when newspapers recounted details of the Zimmerman note. (German Foreign Secretary Alfred Zimmerman's note to the Mexican Government proposed an alliance for making "war together. . . We shall give generous financial support, and it is understood that Mexico is to re-conquer its lost territory in New Mexico, Texas, and Arizona.")

On May 7, 1915, a German U-boat sank the British luxury liner *Lusitania*, resulting in the greatest loss of life in a marine disaster since the *Titanic* had rammed an iceberg three years earlier. More than 1,200 people including 128 Americans lost their lives in the sinking of the *Lusitania*.

Fueled by dramatic accounts in newspapers, most American citizens were outraged, and some, including Former President Theodore Roosevelt, clamored for immediate retaliation. A few were more restrained. Secretary of State Bryan, fervent in his desire not to escalate the war, resigned his position rather than sign a note demanding that Germany abandon submarine warfare, disavow the sinking, and compensate for American lives.

Norris, convinced that the *Lusitania* was carrying munitions, agreed with the Secretary and proclaimed that individuals traveling on an armed ship in time of war were taking the same risks as persons who remained voluntarily in a foreign land while a revolution was underway.

Norris gave strong support to La Follette's strategy in organizing and carrying out a filibuster that would delay any voting by the Senate upon the armed forces bill. The zeal and energy of the dissidents paid off, at least temporarily, for the filibuster successfully delayed voting and the Congressional session adjourned on schedule. One week later, President Wilson, citing an 1819 piracy statute, circumvented the senate by issuing an executive order that called for the arming of merchant ships.

Adding to the arguments, five American ships sailing the North Atlantic were sunk within the next month. The President called for a special session of Congress, and on April 2, 1917, delivered his momentous message asking for a declaration of war.

Senator Norris had not been intimidated when President Wilson had put him among "the little group of willful men" stymieing the government. In the clamor that arose from war hawks in the administration and from citizens across America, no criticism was too wild, no epithet too base. Norris was lumped with La Follette as unpatriotic or perverted — windbags who wanted to drag the flag through the dust and thus dishonor the nation in the eyes of the world.

Two days after the president's request for war, Norris arose in the senate to fire his arrows against the declaration. He contended that the American public had been tricked into a war hysteria by an overwhelming number of newspapers and news agencies in the greatest propaganda the world had ever known. The Nebraskan charged further that the real reason the U.S. was entering the war was because Wall Street had loaned many hundreds of millions of dollars to the Allies, and in calling for war the administration had put "a dollar sign on the American flag."[5]

Congress and most citizens were unmoved by Norris and the few fellow reformists who joined him in speaking against the declaration. When the vote was taken, the House of Representatives approved Wilson's request by a vote of 373 to 50; the final count in the Senate was 82 to 6. Only Senators Robert La Follette, Asle Gronna (N.D.), James Vardaman (Miss.), Harry Lane (Ore.), and William Stone (Mo.), joined with Norris to vote against the measure.

President Wilson returned from his triumphant post war sojourn to Europe bringing with him proposals for America to accept provisions of the Treaty signed at Versailles and its accompanying League of Nations. Henry Cabot Lodge, the senator from Massachusetts dubbed the "scholar in politics," organized and led the fight against both the Treaty and its accompanying League. Norris of Nebraska claimed that because of his votes against the war and his irregularity in party politics, he was not privy to plans Lodge and fellow Republicans made to defeat the proposals.[6]

In July 1919, President Wilson, two days after his return from Europe, personally presented to the Senate for its ratification the twin documents of the Peace Treaty and the League of Nations. The senate's Foreign Relations Committee under its chairman, Senator Lodge, spent the summer holding hearings and debating the measures. Arguments ranged far and wide as tempers rose and accusations abounded.

Meanwhile the mood of American citizens shifted from war-imposed slogans to resentment over the fact that returning soldiers were being discharged with two months' pay, a ticket home, and left to shift for themselves. The longer the senate delayed its voting upon the Treaty and League, the more chance anti-League sentiment was given to expand.

Lodge's committee in ironic recollection of Wilson's Fourteen Points made one reservation after another, and added one, Article X — stipulating that the U.S. would not be obliged to defend any other country at the bidding of the League unless Congress first approved. The wily Lodge knew President Wilson with his dogmatic stubbornness would not accept that reservation.

It was not until November 1919, slightly more than a year after Germany had surrendered, that the Versailles Treaty and the League were voted upon in the U.S. Senate. Norris had reservations, and on the Senate floor he argued against both measures, emphasizing that he was expressing his own judgments independent from party allegiance. When the vote was taken, the Treaty and the League were defeated 55 to 39.

Once America entered the hostilities of World War I, notwithstanding his hatred of war, Norris had supported the military programs. He never recanted from his assertions, however, that America had gotten into that war through a tricky crusade and with unholy reasons. He was not a dyed-in-the-wool pacifist dedicated to abandon all for that cause, and when he saw the rise of militant dictatorships in Germany and Japan during the 1930s, his opposition to armament and to U.S. involvement in world affairs eroded.

In the interval between the two major world wars, Norris gave most of his attention to domestic matters. He had withstood the criticisms fired at him during the World War I crisis and through moral courage and steadfastness had attained political leadership in the senate. One of his most significant achievements was enactment of the so-called Lame Duck measure — the 20th Amendment to the American Constitution.

This relatively simple change had a long, tortuous, ten-year history before Norris successfully guided it over parliamentary hurdles in Congress. Under terms in the document prepared by the Constitutional Convention meeting in Philadelphia in 1787, the terms of President and the Vice President were set at four years; terms of senators at six years, and members of the House of Representatives at two years. A year later, early agreement among members attending the Congress of the Confederation in 1788 had fixed the date on which the new American government should begin to operate: the first Wednesday in March, 1789. Those decisions established a long session of Congress and a short one — the latter commonly called the lame duck session.

Members elected to the House of Representatives in a November election could not enter upon their duties until the following March, and in that month the short session of Congress would adjourn until its resumption in December. For all practical purposes, all representatives and one third of the senators were not sworn into office until approximately thirteen months after their election.

In 1923, Senator Norris tried to correct the thwarting of what he maintained was popular will as shown by election results when he submitted his first resolution to quash the short, unproductive, lame duck session. For ten years, the simple, common sense reform measure was voted down by members of Congress or shunted aside into mountainous piles of agenda items.

One of Norris's antagonists was Speaker of the House Nicholas Longworth. Although not as powerful as Joseph Cannon (who once had ruled the chamber), Longworth could maneuver around many undesired proposals, and as a conservative Republican he considered that anything coming from this Nebraskan maverick would be positively dangerous.[7]

For ten years Speaker Longworth had managed to bottle up Norris's attempts to get a resolution combining the elimination of the electoral college and remedying the defect in dates of service by Representatives. Norris by 1923 had been persuaded to drop elimination of the electoral college from his resolution when he submitted it in December, 1922, and when the senate voted upon it two months later it passed with a tally of 63 to 6. His moral conviction and determination again had paid off.

President Calvin Coolidge in 1928 announced he did not "choose to run," and the Republican Party Convention nominated Herbert Clark Hoover in his stead. Norris voiced his displeasure at the choice by saying that both the platform and the candidate adopted at the Kansas City meeting of Republicans would be "a sad disappointment to every progressive citizen of the United States."

Norris, still a nominal Republican, broke ranks, threw party allegiance aside, and supported Democratic nominee Alfred E. Smith. Norris's constituency back in Nebraska was rural, "dry," and Protestant; Smith was urban, "wet," and Catholic, but in the judgment of Norris, Smith was morally right in wanting to rein in the great trusts controlling the nation's railroads and natural resources.

Norris' third term expired in 1930, and in running for a fourth one he was subjected to the hardest and most acrimonious campaign in his career. Nevertheless, he withstood the slurs and won re-election in a year when the Great Depression was worsening. Outright foes charged he was a drunkard, an immoral wretch, and throughout regions dominated by the Ku Klux Klan it was rumored that he had a Catholic wife. Old guard Republicans accused him of bolting the party in order to support secretly the candidacy of Democrat Franklin D. Roosevelt. At first, Norris denied the last named accusation but then hedged by saying he thought "Roosevelt was the best man to fight the power trust."[8]

The Great Depression proved to be fertile ground for worsening relations between labor and management, and nowhere were feelings more intense than in coal mining regions. In those regions, particularly Pennsylvania, working conditions were deplorable, and management leaders fought organized labor intensely. Gradually, there had developed what was known as the "yellow dog contract," which in effect asked a laborer to surrender his rights to ask for increased wages, for better working conditions, or to associate with fellow workers who were doing so. Furthermore, he had to promise not to join a labor union.

When disputes arose, courts generally ruled more favorably toward the operators of coal mines than the miners who actually dug the coal out of the ground. Norris, after a personal inspection trip throughout Pennsylvania and other coal mining regions, felt that through these yellow dog contracts, thousands of miners were compelled to work under conditions too horrible for a free country. Accordingly, he introduced a bill in the senate which would make the yellow dog contract illegal. In the House of Representatives a brash newcomer from New York, Fiorello La Guardia, submitted a companion bill. Both bills were defeated the first time presented, but in the next session of Congress when Norris and La Guardia submitted them again, the mood of the country had swung in favor of the miners, and in March, 1932, Congress voted favorably on the Anti-Injunction Act, more commonly referred to as the Norris–La Guardia Act, named for its sponsors.

Norris was proud of his role in getting the legislation passed and would write,

This law is labor's charter — to be guarded and protected against attack from without and from within. . . Labor in the mines, labor everywhere, should be free from contractual relationships in its employment that strip the individual of the rights of American citizenship. The charter for labor embraced in this legislation gave labor no right than any American ought not to possess in his daily life and in his day in court. [9]

Before the 1932 Democratic Convention began in Chicago, Norris was forthright and had declared his support for the man who would become their nominee, Franklin Delano Roosevelt. President Herbert Hoover, running for reelection, had accepted the Republican nomination, and as the campaign got underway Norris condemned Hoover for being out of step on "every vital issue confronting the nation."

After Roosevelt's landslide win, capturing 472 electoral votes out of the available 531 from the 48 states, Norris continued to support the victor and his platform. After years of arid Republican domination in White House and Congress, the new administration was a giant improvement. Norris was in agreement with most of the programs under the New Deal, but he did not embrace Roosevelt's moves toward building a cohesive political party. The Nebraska senator had no regrets about forsaking his own party and casting his lot with FDR, for as late as 1935, he stated, ". . . the last two years . . . produced more social legislation than any two since he had come to Washington."[10]

Seldom is a single individual solely responsible for great achievements. True, Robert Fulton developed the steamboat, Eli Whitney the cotton gin, and Cyrus McCormick the reaper, but all built their achievements on the findings and work of forerunners. The Louisiana Purchase came after a decision by Thomas Jefferson; the building of the Panama Canal might not have been done had it not been for Teddy Roosevelt, and the first airplane flight is credited to Wilbur and Orville Wright. In these and other such instances, the achievement is an amalgam of efforts and ambitions of persons who contributed knowledge and shared goals of the man or woman usually given credit.

Franklin Roosevelt is most often praised for creating the Tennessee Valley Authority established during his first term in office. Surely, it is no detraction from FDR to point out that others played indispensable roles in creating TVA, and certainly no one individual was more important in its creation than Senator George Norris.

During the First World War, the U.S. Government had built a large hydroelectric power plant and two munitions factories at Muscle Shoals on the Tennessee River in the northwest corner of Alabama. For fifteen years afterward, various administrations had tried unsuccessfully to dispose of the Muscle Shoals facilities to private interests.

The Tennessee River is formed by the confluence of other rivers arising in South Carolina and southwestern Virginia. Fed also by smaller streams on the west slope of the Appalachians, the Tennessee flows southwestward past Knoxville, Chattanooga, and Chickamauga into northern Alabama. In the years before 1933, the 652-mile-long river ran through a valley with heavier rainfall than any other region of the U.S. except the Pacific Northwest; it was subjected to disastrous floods, denuding the land with devastating effects upon families trying to scratch out a living.

The impoverished area had been stripped of timber after the Civil War, and in the twentieth century more than a million families in the barren land were living on a diet of corn meal and salt pork. One could go to towns like Savannah, Tennessee, or Decatur, Alabama, and see countless children, ragged, under-nourished, and vacant-eyed. Land was sold for the taxes owed, and a third of the population had malaria, tuberculosis, pellagra, or trachoma. Half the valley's population lived on farms, and 97 per cent of those farms had no electricity.

Throughout the hectic "Hundred Days," Norris remained impressed with the aristocrat from Hyde Park, and a month after moving into the White House the new President wrote him a letter expressing the hope to get a bill through Congress,

> ... which would allow us to spend $25 million this year to put 25,000 families on farms at an average cost of $1,000 per family. It can be done... Will you talk this over with some of your fellow dreamers on the hill?[11]

Norris, who linked the hard times of the 1880s with the depression years of the 1930s, had talked often of the one great central problem — the use of the earth for the good of man — and the President's suggestion gave him an outlet for his dream.

Roosevelt invited Norris to accompany him on an inspection trip through the region, and on that trip and other occasions the two discussed upgrading Muscle Shoals as well as developing the entire Tennessee Basin. On March 9, 1933, the day the first session of the Seventy-third Congress convened, Senator Norris introduced a joint resolution calling for development of the Tennessee Valley.

It was May before the Muscle Shoals project became a main order of business on the agenda of the U.S. Senate. Speaking as usual without notes, Norris used three days to describe the poverty-stricken area and living conditions for the valley's families. Then he launched into benefits to be derived from the giant project — improved living conditions and better health for residents, flood control, and river navigation — but he devoted most of his time to the benefits of power. Dams once built could provide power for electricity to aid industries and light the darkened homes.

Similar bills were presented in the House of Representatives, and both chambers voted that the proposals be referred to a joint committee. By May 8, 1933, the conferees had reached agreement. A week later the conference report, labeled the Norris–Hill bill for Operation of Muscle Shoals and Development of the Tennessee Valley, passed the Senate without debate or a roll call. The next day the House likewise gave it overwhelming endorsement.

Estimated cost of a dam to be built at Cove Creek, Tennessee, twenty miles north of Knoxville, was $31 million, and engineers anticipated it would take four years to complete the project. (The engineers were wrong, and the dam was completed two years ahead of schedule.)

On August 1, 1933, the Tennessee Valley Authority announced that the dam yet to be constructed would bear the name "Norris Dam," honoring the senator whose dreams it had fulfilled.[12]

Within a period of less than two years, George Norris had slipped the shackles of party discipline and had guided through the Senate three very significant measures: the anti-injunction bill, his "lame duck" amendment, and now the Muscles Shoals bill. He would regard this last as "the most significant legislation" placed on the statute books since he had been in public life.

The Great Depression had not run its full course by 1935 as George Norris began planning his campaign for a fourth term in the Senate. Drought, dust storms, and grasshoppers in his home state kept adding to the woes of farmers and townspeople there who were grappling with the crisis. In that year, 90% of America's farmers relied on horses, mules, hand labor, and gas engines for power. Without benefits of electricity, farmers toiled in a nineteenth-century world; their wives performed back-breaking chores much like peasant women in medieval Europe. In the evening, a wife might snatch a moment under a kerosene lamp to eye enviously pictures in *Colliers* or the *Saturday Evening Post* of city women with washing machines, refrigerators, or vacuum cleaners.

The New Deal Congress in April 1935 had established an Emergency Relief Appropriation Act giving the President authority to create an agency which would make funds available for low-cost, long-term loans which were to be spent for rural electrification. In the next year, George Norris with encouragement and backing from President Roosevelt helped add this temporary agency to the permanent apparatus of government.

In early 1936, Norris presented his measure to the Senate calling for permanent establishment of the Rural Electrification Act. Under its provision would be an annual appropriation of $100 million to be spent for three specific purposes: rural transmission lines, electric appliances, and electrification of farm homes. As usual, there was a bevy of amendments, delays, and blockages before a conference committee of Representatives and Senators could report a bill overcoming minor objections. Both chambers passed the bill, and the Rural Electrification Administration became law giving the agency the power to build power lines and finance electricity production in areas not served by private distributors. Another Norris dream had come about, and another laurel added to his crown.

There were occasional disagreements with the Administration, but in 1936 Norris supported FDR for re-election; he in turn publicly praised the courageous senator from the opposition party. Even in the bitter controversy over enlargement of the Supreme Court, Republican Norris stood with the Democratic president.

During the "Hundred Days" of Franklin Roosevelt's first administration, hurriedly passed legislation like the Emergency Banking Act, the Economic Act, and abandonment of the Gold Standard had helped shore up financial institutions. Broader authority was needed, however, and FDR with the aid of Democratic stalwarts prepared a bill called the nation's Economic Recovery Act. When the bill was approved by Congress and became law, a National Recovery Administration (NRA) was established. Programs under this banner (the Blue Eagle) became one of the New Deal's most touted and controversial elements.

Purposes of the NRA were to revive industrial and business activity and reduce unemployment — the most visible sores of the Great Depression. The high-minded NRA was begun with new fair trade codes to be approved by the President and enforceable by law.

Business leaders saw the broad powers of the NRA as intrusions upon their basic rights, and adverse reactions mounted; even some old guard New Dealers broke ranks. Eventually, a legal case created national repercussions as it percolated its way to the Supreme Court. The Court, the nation's highest legal authority, brushed aside arguments of the administration and in a unanimous decision ruled that in approving the National Recovery Act, Congress had exceeded its authority.

An embittered President Roosevelt claimed the Court had reduced modern government to "the horse and buggy age." His denigration made the bubbling stew boil over. Buoyed by the size of his victory in winning reelection in that November of 1936, FDR was ready to continue the fight. He sought advice from his Attorney General Homer Cummings, and together they developed a plan whereby the President would be authorized to appoint a new judge for every federal judge who remained on the bench six months after reaching the age of seventy. The Supreme Court was not to exceed fifteen and not more than fifty new judges would be added to the lower courts.

Hostile reactions from both liberals and conservatives were immediate and fervent. Senator Burton Wheeler advocated instead a form of recall in which Congress by a two-thirds vote could nullify judicial decisions; Senator Borah offered the idea that the Fourteenth Amendment should be revised so that states would be granted all powers which the Supreme Court denied the federal government. Norris of Nebraska proposed a two-part reform: first, Congress should pass a law requiring a two-thirds vote by the Supreme Court to invalidate an act of Congress, and second, a constitutional amendment would establish a definite nine-year term for the entire federal judiciary. All three plans were voted down by the Judiciary Committee of the Senate. The President's bill was reported by the Committee but with a negative recommendation.

Norris had lost his battle, and despite all of FDR's political acumen, his attempt to enlarge the Court had failed. Yet on this momentous issue, the senator from Nebraska had again defied party regulars to join their Democratic rivals.

As his third senatorial term was approaching its end in 1930, Norris told Republican Party managers he was ready to retire, saying that he had become the target of organized wealth and entrenched selfish interests. Under no circumstances would he accept re-nomination as a Republican candidate, and he would not even consider being a Democrat nominee.

Six years later, in the summer of 1936, the Nebraska countryside was as brown and sear as in late fall. Daytime temperatures soared, ranging day after day well above 100 degrees. Associates loyal to Norris would not accept his refusal to run and began collecting signatures for an independent candidacy. Presented with more than 41,000 signatures on the petitions, Norris agreed to run as an Independent.

When the election was held, he triumphed by a substantial margin over both Republican and Democratic rivals. Thus Norris broke his formal ties with both of the two major political parties, and he would be recognized as an Independent throughout the rest of his career.

In 1942, George Norris at the age of eighty-one waged his last campaign. He recognized that odds were against him, but loyalist supporters filed more than 15,000 signatures in endorsement if he would run. America had entered the war, more than 60,000 Nebraskans were in the armed services, and thousands of farmers along with a multitude of others had left the state seeking work in defense plants.

Norris ran as an Independent from Nebraska, a state where political allegiances had fractured. Neither major party in the state was as divided as they had been in the 1930s, though Democratic leadership was discredited and Republicans focused attention on in-fighting over patronage. Liberalism in Nebraska was on the wane, with the New Deal and Roosevelt taking the brunt of the criticism. Most newspapers in the state did not endorse Norris for his fifth Senate run, and he said he doubted if any Republicans in Congress would endorse him. He was wrong, for beyond the state, the clamor in his favor rose. President Roosevelt gave public praise, and congressional colleagues of every persuasion expressed hopes that he would be re-elected.

The farther one got from Nebraska, the more ecstatic were comments on his candidacy. Most newspapers in Nebraska did not join the national groundswell; one exception was the *Lincoln Star*, whose editor James Lawrence was Norris's campaign manager.

In this campaign and in contrast to earlier ones, foes no longer vehemently denounced him. Even the bitterest ones recognized his stature as an elder statesman; instead they concentrated upon his age and his apostasies in supporting Roosevelt and the New Deal. The eyes of the nation were on Nebraska as its citizens went to the polls on November 3, 1942. Two days earlier a group of reporters with long experience in Washington placed an advertisement in the *Omaha-World Herald* asking Nebraska voters to return Norris to the Senate. On the same date, the *New York Times* in a brief dispatch predicted a Norris defeat.[13]

After casting his vote in Nebraska, Norris boarded a train for Chicago and from there went back to Washington. He was on familiar stomping grounds when his daughter gave the bad news: he had been defeated in the Republican landslide throughout the Midwest. Norris had trailed his rival, regular Republican Kenneth S. Wherry, in all but three of Nebraska's ninety-three counties. One newspaper in Washington reported that "The Dean of the Senate has been tumbled in the worst rebuff the New Deal has received, though it has not lost control of Congress.[14]

A shocked and embittered George Norris explained his defeat by alleging that citizens in his home state had deserted him because of his record in helping bring about so many measures of the New Deal. Voters in his state simply did not like the New Deal, and he added,

> There seems to be a universal hatred among a lot of our people against Roosevelt. . . In the campaign, nothing was said by the opposition against me. Even my two opponents when they mentioned me or referred to me, did it with praise and commendation. . . . The most important thing is that righteousness has been crucified and the people I love have condemned the things I held most sacred; personally I find it a repudiation of forty years of service.[15]

When his final term in the Senate ended, Norris and his wife abandoned their apartment in Washington and returned to Nebraska. Before leaving the capital city he was offered the position of chairman of the Tennessee Valley Board, but even after getting encouragement from President Roosevelt he turned down the offer.

Recognized everywhere as America's elder statesman, George Norris was in great demand. In the next year and a half, he gave major speeches at Carnegie Hall in New York City, at testimonial dinners in his honor at the Mayflower Hotel in Washington and another at the Commodore Hotel in New York City as well as addresses in Chicago, Boston, and Washington, D.C. The speeches were broadcast over the major radio networks and were reported extensively in the nation's newspapers. The war was being fought in Europe and throughout the Pacific area, so Norris made frequent references to ideals which had sent Americans into action. His reputation swelled to its highest levels.

He wanted to settle down in McCook and begin writing his memoirs, but invitations to speak kept coming in unabated. It was hard to refuse such acknowledgments, so his writing slowed as he traveled through Nebraska and the Midwest to meet the obligations. Everywhere he went, he was met with friendly receptions, but traveling and speaking took their toll.

The Christmas season of 1943 found him busy with his autobiography and keeping abreast in his work as senator-at-large. On two separate occasions during that year he made public pronouncements concerning the forthcoming presidential election, and in both instances endorsed Franklin Roosevelt for a fourth term. In the last year of his life, Norris paid increased attention to race relations and to world peace. Concern for civil rights was getting more public attention, and his desire to find a path for world peace was as strong as ever.

February 1944 was a bad month for him. Weather kept him indoors, and he finished writing his autobiography in April, 1944. Primary elections were approaching, and he didn't hesitate to express his anti-feelings for candidates who opposed the President and his policies.

As Democrats prepared for their nominating convention scheduled to be held in Chicago, Norris back in Nebraska was certain Roosevelt would be the nominee. He was not so sure about the second place. Norris couldn't accept James Byrnes, the so-called Assistant President, because of Byrnes's Southern upbringing and anti-labor positions; he knew little about Senator Harry Truman but had been impressed by the zeal and thoroughness the Missourian had displayed in chairing the Senate Committee to Investigate the War Effort. Although he knew that many powerful factions opposed Henry A. Wallace, Norris indisputably favored him because of the attitude Wallace "had taken all along in brave and courageous support of principles that progressives everywhere believe in."

In that election year, almost every topic or issue in some way touched upon the presidential campaign, but Norris did not focus upon it entirely. He was distressed by a transit strike in Philadelphia, for instance, because he said the strikers there apparently were "not moved in any degree by the spirit of patriotism." In another matter, he reiterated his conviction that the Negro should be protected in his right to vote without pressures or coercion.

In McCook, Nebraska, the vigor and robust health of George Norris failed, and on Monday, August 28th, he suffered a cerebral hemorrhage, never regaining full consciousness. Five days later, on September 2, 1944, the doughty champion of liberal causes — a progressive who would not let party allegiance deter him from sponsoring moves to improve the democracy he cherished — passed away quietly in his home town.

Chronology of George William Norris

Born . . . July 11, 1861 in York Township, Sandusky County, Ohio

Parents . . . Chauncey Norris and Mary Magdalene Norris

Education . . . Country school at Mt. Carmel, Ohio, Baldwin College (Berea, Ohio); Graduated and Received LLB from Northern Indiana Normal (later Valparaiso University) in Valparaiso, Indiana . . . 1883

Moved to Beaver City, Nebraska . . . 1885

Married Pluma Lashely . . . 1889

Family: George and Pluma Norris had three daughters

District Judge in Nebraska . . . 1895–1902

Married Ellie Leonard . . . 1903

Congressman, Nebraska's 5th Congressional District. . . 1903–1912

Led House Revolt Against Speaker Joseph Cannon . . . 1910

Helped Form the National Progressive Republican League . . . 1911

Supported the Bull Moose Movement . . . 1912

U.S. Senator from Nebraska . . . 1913–1943

Voted Against Declaration of War . . . 1917

Teamed with La Follette & Progressives . . . 1917–1923

Led in Adoption of the Lame Duck Amendment . . . December 1922

Helped Defeat Ratification of Versailles Treaty and League of Nations . . . 1919

Bolted Republican Party & Supported Democrat Alfred E. Smith . . . 1928

Bolted Republican Party to Support Democrat Franklin D. Roosevelt . . .1932

Sponsor of La Guardia Anti-Injunction Act . . . 1933

Sponsor of the 20th (Lame Duck) Amendment to Federal Constitution . . . 1933

Leader in Passage of Tennessee Valley Authority Act . . . May 18, 1933

Senate Leader for Rural Electrification Act, Passed, May 18, 1935

Supported FDR's Plan for Supreme Court Revision . . . 1936

Left Republican Party & Reelected to Senate as an Independent . . . 1936

Defeated in Bid for 6th Term in Senate . . . 1942

Died . . . McCook, Nebraska . . . September 2, 1944

Chapter 6. Henry Agard Wallace: New Deal Reformist

In the year of 1887, Theodore Roosevelt gave up his land holdings in the Dakota Territory, and twelve months later he finished putting his western experiences into a book entitled *Ranch Life and the Hunting Trail* (with Frederic Remington. New York: The Century Company, 1888). Iowa, having become a state 43 years earlier, was not as wild as the land TR wrote about; nevertheless, Adair County, midway between Des Moines and Council Bluffs, was still primitive compared to areas east of the Mississippi.

Little more than a village, the town of Orient lay almost on the southern line of Adair County, and on a farm near that hamlet Henry Agard Wallace was born on October 7, 1888. That part of the county was almost devoid of trees, but it had good, fertile soil that gave birth to acres of Bluestem grass, and scattered fields of wheat, rye, or corn. Madison County to the east was more prosperous, better forested, and boasted a larger population.

Henry A. Wallace was named after his paternal grandfather, Reverend Henry Wallace, an important figure in Adair County — major landholder, publisher of a local newspaper, and editor of the state's most influential farm journal. As was customary, Reverend Wallace's first son was named after him, but soon and for most of his life he would be called Harry in part to distinguish him from the father. When he was twenty-one years old, Harry met May Brodhead then living in Muscatine, Iowa. The courtship began, and the two were married on Thanksgiving Day, November 24, 1887.

The couple moved into a modest dwelling on three hundred treeless acres near Orient and began their farming careers. The acreage — nothing much — but it had a story-and-a-half house as well as a windmill. The property was owned by Reverend Wallace, who leased all of it to his son and daughter-in-law. Harry, in efforts to make the treeless plains more attractive, planted catalpa, maple, and plum trees and a small apple orchard He hoped to make the farm profitable by raising purebred shorthorn cattle, Poland China hogs, Percheron horses, and feeder cattle.

In 1888, by the time the ground thawed in late spring, May Wallace was pregnant with her first child. The couple had chosen bad times to start farming. The price of corn went down each year, but hog prices didn't rise accordingly. Corn which in 1883 had sold for .32 cents per bushel brought only .24 cents five years later, and in the next year had dropped to .19 cents — its lowest level in decades. Prices for cattle and hogs suffered similar declines.

Bad luck seemed to plague all the farmers in the county, and it hit Harry and May Wallace especially hard. Cholera broke out among their hogs; purebred shorthorns had to be sold to meet expenses, and remaining cattle were sold for less than $100 per head — one third of what they had cost. After five years of struggling, Harry and May were ready to admit their farming adventure was failing; they just couldn't make it.

Harry decided to return to Iowa State College to finish his education. He and May bundled up their two children — four-year-old Henry Agard and one-year-old Annabelle — and moved to Ames, where they lived in a tiny house adjacent to the Northwestern railroad tracks. The home was almost unbearable in the torrid heat of summer and fall, and during other seasons the place was whipped by cold and fierce winds. The sound of window panes shaking in the freeze of a winter evening would always remind Henry Agard of Ames, Iowa.[1]

Harry, young Henry's father, was appointed an associate professor at Ames, where his duties brought him into contact with George Washington Carver. Carver, the son of former slaves, had wandered through the Midwest after the Civil War and was the first black student at the Ames college, earning a master's degree before moving to Tuskegee Institute in Alabama.

Carver often was in the Wallace home either for dinner or as a guest invited to share an evening with a colleague. Thus Henry Agard saw Carver frequently; they shared a love for plants, and took nature walks together, stopping to let Carver explain to the lad more about a particular species and its characteristics. It cannot be said that the two were buddies — the age differential was too great for that — but young Henry recognized Carver's expertise, and Carver appreciated the boy's probing questions, his trenchant observations about plants, and his promise of scientific inquiry. Years later Henry Wallace would recall:

> . . . He [Carver] took a fancy to me and took me with him on his botanizing expeditions. . . I remember him claiming to my father that I had greatly surprised him by recognizing the pistils and stamens of redrop, a kind of grass. . . the mere fact of his boasting, I think, incited me to learn more than if I had really done what he said I had done.[2]

May Wallace, Henry's mother, had taught her son even while very young to crossbreed pansies, producing offspring which although unremarkable he considered his own creation. Plants of all sorts continued to fascinate him, and chief among them was King Corn. When his father Harry moved the family to the western edge of Des Moines, young Henry established a garden of his own, raising enough tomatoes, cabbages, celery, and other vegetables to feed the family.

Corn was the most important crop produced by American farmers, and even before he became a teenager, corn had become a dominant interest in Henry A. Wallace's life. It was a fascinating plant for a young man with a scientific bent and who already was experimenting with strawberries and garden vegetables. For centuries, tillers who raised corn simply selected the best looking ears to keep for seeding the next year's planting. Throughout the Midwest, farm interests developed a trend for "corn shows," wherein ears of corn were judged according to their appearance — size, evenness of rows, kernels, color, etc.

In Iowa at that time, an acknowledged expert for judging in the corn shows was Perry G. Holden — part teacher, part salesman, and all showman. In 1904 Holden offered a short course at Iowa State College, and fifteen-year-old Henry A. Wallace attended. He listened carefully as he watched Holden extol the message of good farming and explain the usual criteria for judging the yellow ears of corn. But the lad was not fully persuaded, for Holden said nothing about the size of the yield, and it was yield — not beauty or symmetry of the corn ears — that should be the farmer's benchmark. Henry asked himself, "What does it matter how corn looks to a hungry hog?"

When challenged, Holden reasserted his belief that good appearance of the ears should be the farmer's goal, and if his brash questioner doubted that goal he could test the theory himself: the finest looking ears would produce the biggest yields and the worst looking ones would produce the smallest yields. Holden was willing to give young Wallace thirty-three ears of Reid's Yellow Dent — the most widely-accepted breed of corn at the time.

Henry took the thirty-three ears back to the farm near Johnston, and in the spring he planted kernels from each ear in two separate rows. He knew enough about plants to understand that he had to eliminate any possibility of self-fertilization, so he decided to detassel half his crop, that is, to cut off the corn plant's male element — the tassel — so that it could not reproduce itself. In the fall, he husked the ears and stored them in three hundred neatly numbered piles. Then he waited until the ears had dried and could be shelled and weighed. He calculated the percentage of an ear composed of grain kernels and estimated the weight lost through drying.

In summarizing his results, Henry found that the fine Reid's Yellow Dent ears that Professor Holden had given him ranged in yield from thirty-three to seventy-nine bushels an acre. Some of the best-yielding ears were those Holden had said were the poorest, and the ear Holden had judged to be best of them all was one of the ten worst in yield. Throughout the Midwest, Holden continued to be called upon as an expert in corn farming, yet young Henry Wallace had torpedoed the professor's theory of the crop's propagation.

Intrigued by his findings, Henry went further, and studied and developed his math skills so that he could better tabulate and translate his observations of several generations of corn he raised in his experimental plots. His studies in genetics had introduced him to the findings of Gregor Mendel, the Austrian scientist who through his growing of peas found that separate characteristics (e.g., height, vigor, resistance, etc.) in a plant can be passed on independently of one another. This fundamental fact would be Wallace's benchmark as he raised his generations of corn.

Wallace came to understand that each reproductive cell receives only one of a pair of alternative factors (factors such as tallness, vigor, or resistance) existing in the other body of cells. The factor received in the reproductive cell is the *dominant* gene, but it will also carry other factors known as *recessive* ones. When individuals purebred in respect to one characters showing *dominance* are crossed with purebred individuals showing the alternate characters, the hybrid offspring will show the dominant character, but its cells also will carry the *recessive* factors. A crossing of these hybrids gives an average of one out of four individuals bearing two *dominant* factors, one bearing two *recessive* factors, and two bearing both factors. Therefore, the offspring of hybrids exhibit the *dominant* character as a ratio of three to one. In succeeding generations the contrasting characters sort out and appear in the offspring in ratios predictable according to Mendelian laws of heredity. It was Henry Wallace's grasp and understanding of these facts that guided him through his corn research and to his fame as a scientist who would change the agricultural pattern not only in America but in the entire world.

Wallace already was involved with corn experiments when he entered Iowa State College in 1906. The institution then was still pretty much of a "cow college." One third of its students were either agriculture or veterinary majors. Plant life was Henry's passion, but he chose to major in animal husbandry. Just as in high school, he found many required courses unfulfilling, and he constantly challenged some tenets being taught. One professor recalled that Wallace was a thinker anxious to spend time discussing a particular matter of teaching. Said the professor, "As I think of it now, he was half a jump ahead of the instructors in some classes."[3]

At the end of his junior year at Iowa State, Henry began his career as a journalist — a calling he would follow for the next quarter of a century. First, he traveled in the West, sending back reports written in plain, non-poetic prose. His submissions ranged from dogie branding in Texas to irrigation projects in Kansas.

He returned to Ames for his senior year and graduated from Iowa State College in June 1910, at the top of the college's agricultural division. By that year, the ideals and achievements of his grandfather Reverend Henry Wallace along with the status of his father, now called Harry Wallace and a close advisor to Gifford Pinchot in President Taft's administration, had elevated the family's name.

Henry A. Wallace, after graduating from college, became a full-time writer and editor of *Wallace's Farmer*, the weekly magazine Grandfather Henry had started in 1896. The ten years following the start of the magazine brought good fortune to the Wallace family. The financial panic that had swept the country during Grover Cleveland's second administration eased, and farm prices began moving upwards. Corn that had brought fourteen cents per bushel in 1896 could be sold for fifty-two cents per bushel five years later.

The Wallaces were believers in the educational values of travel, and in 1912 the family funded a journey for Henry which took him first to Washington, D.C., and then to Europe visiting agricultural figures in France, Holland, Belgium, and Germany.

Upon his return in the next year, good fortune continued to smile on him when he met Ilo Browne at an evening picnic in Des Moines. Ilo's round pretty face and her sparkling brown eyes, wavy brown hair, and radiant smile captivated Henry at once. The couple went on frequent buggy rides, often gossiping about plants — tomatoes, strawberries, and especially corn — before May, 1914, when they married in Des Moines in a ceremony conducted by Reverend Henry Wallace.

In the third week of May, 1926, newspapers blazoned with headlines about the kidnapping of Aimee Semple MacPherson, sensational revivalist who had attracted huge crowds throughout California. Her sudden, mysterious reappearance led the district attorney of Los Angeles to launch an investigation, and from it he branded the kidnapping a hoax, setting off a national controversy. Even after all criminal charges against her had been dropped, MacPherson carried her case to enthusiastic audiences at home and abroad.

Back in Des Moines, Henry Wallace was not among those enthralled with MacPherson's escapade, for at about the same time her story broke he had called together associates who met with him in a Des Moines hotel. The meeting was unheralded, but would become far more important to the nation's welfare than the reported kidnapping.

The men in Wallace's meeting were J. J. Newlin, a Quaker who managed the Wallace farm north of Des Moines, Simon Cassady, apple grower and small scale developer, Fred Lehman, Jr., an abrasive young lawyer, Walter Welch, a salesman, George Kurtzweil, seed salesman, Earl Houghton, a neighboring farmer, and Jim Wallace, Henry A.'s younger brother.

The disparate men were a little shaky when it came to understanding the genetics Wallace tried to explain, but all of them shared respect and faith in the young man and his vision. At first, he failed to realize the potential in the commercialization of hybrid corn; all he wanted was to get the information out to farmers so that they could reap better corn yields. He aimed to hold institutes and short courses to spread his findings, but his colleagues soon convinced him those measures would not be enough. There ought to be an organization which could market, sell, and deliver the hybrid seed as well as maintain plots to provide more seed to improve succeeding generations.

Wallace was persuaded and drew up a shareholder plan along with incorporation papers. Pioneer Hi-Bred would be the corporate name and there were to be seventy shares. (Because of competition from a small seed company in North Dakota, Wallace's corporation did not obtain rights to the trademark name Pioneer Hi-Bred until 1959.) Wallace himself would hold fifty shares, and his friends agreed to buy the other twenty.

Another person who helped make the new corporation possible was not in attendance. That person was Ilo, Wallace's wife who was home minding the children; it was the inheritance she received from her father's estate that provided most of the initial funds to set up Pioneer Hi-Bred Company.[4]

No one, and certainly not Henry or Ilo Wallace, could foresee the enormous success of Hi-Bred Seed Corn. The company started slowly, and in its first years, profits, if any, were meager — a few hundred dollars. Gradually though, Wallace was assembling a team of experts — men who could market and sell his seed corn as well as ones who could manage the constant cross-breeding on research plots north of Des Moines.

A man largely responsible for promoting Pioneer Hi-Bred Seed Corn in the Midwest was Roswell Garst of Coon Rapids, Iowa. Initially, Wallace had given Garst some seed corn to plant, and when during the growing season a violent windstorm knocked down all the rows of regular corn that Garst had planted but left stalks from the seed corn plantings upright and healthy, Garst became a believer.

On nothing more than a handshake, he and Wallace agreed on a limited partnership: Wallace would supply the hybrid seed and Garst would sell it, paying the company a royalty for each bushel sold. Moving from farm to farm, Garst gave a farmer enough Pioneer Hi-Bred seed to plant alongside the farmer's regular sowings. If the farmer's regular seed yielded twenty-five bushels to the acre — considered then an average yield — and the hybrid seed produced forty-five bushels, Garst would be entitled to half the increase, i.e., ten bushels of corn. It sometimes took three or more years to convince a farmer, but the increases were unmistakable. All three — farmer, Garst, and especially Wallace — profited enormously.

In late 1931 and early 1932, two representatives from a coterie of followers Franklin D. Roosevelt was building were sent to Iowa to visit Henry Wallace. The two men, Rexford Guy Tugwell and Henry Morgenthau, Jr., came separately, but each was favorably impressed by Wallace.

Franklin Roosevelt was building his political base, and he encouraged Morgenthau to invite the maverick farm leader to come to Hyde Park for a meeting. Thus Wallace, the Iowa editor who had supported Al Smith in 1928 but was a registered Republican and son of Republican President Harding's

Secretary of Agriculture, met the scion of a prominent Eastern family and a Democrat who would become the nation's 32nd president, serving in that office longer than any of his predecessors.

The meeting FDR held with Henry Wallace was scheduled to last half an hour, but it stretched into more than two, and in what must have been music to Wallace's ears, FDR talked about the value of a "shelter belt" of trees stretching across the Great Plains. From there, he shared his plans to improve farmland he had bought in Georgia. When Wallace got an opportunity to talk, he described the plight of farmers in the Midwest beset by drought, dust storms, low prices, and high mortgages. He brought up tenancy problems he had seen in the South and discussed solutions that had been applied in England and Ireland.

Wallace would deny that at this meeting anything was said about a cabinet appointment if Roosevelt were to be elected. The Iowan said, "We didn't discuss the election or the campaign at all. Not an iota. No politics, as such, came up at all that day."[5]

Wallace returned to Iowa and threw himself into Roosevelt's campaign for the presidency. Editor Wallace declared in *Wallace's Farmer*, "With Roosevelt, farmers have a chance — I shall vote for Roosevelt." The election in that fall of 1932 was a rout; FDR amassed 22.8 million popular votes to 15.7 million for his opponent Herbert Hoover.

Several days after the election, Wallace received a phone call from Raymond Moley, a Columbia University professor who was leading a group around FDR known familiarly as his Brain Trust. Moley relayed the message that FDR, presently at Warm Springs, Georgia, enjoying a respite after the strenuous campaign, wanted to see Wallace as soon as possible.

Wallace packed his bags and made the trip by train to Georgia. There he was given opportunities for long talks with Moley and Morgenthau and was among those who gathered around FDR for snacks and cocktails. Wallace abstained from the cocktails but listened intently to jovial exchanges and remarks from FDR or members in attendance. Nothing was said about a cabinet appointment, but Wallace understood that his presence meant he had been admitted to a network of close advisors to the new President.

The formal offer of a cabinet position reached Wallace on February 6, 1933, when he had returned to Des Moines after giving a speech to mortgage lenders in Omaha. The message from FDR read, "I want to have the privilege of having you as an official member of my family in the post as Secretary of Agriculture." The message continued by asking Wallace to reply by radio to the yacht *Nourmahal*, via the Navy's communication office.

In memoirs, Wallace said he hesitated, but within a day or two he wrote a formal response to his new boss still fishing aboard Vincent Astor's yacht:

> Your invitation can have but one reply. I appreciate the honor and accept the responsibility. So far as it is in me, I will carry my part of the "family burdens."[6]

During the first "Hundred Days," the new president, his cabinet, and all members of his administration were extremely busy. Legislative and executive landmarks came in quick succession:

March 9 - Emergency Banking Act

March 20 - Economy Act

March 31 - Civilian Conservation Corps

April 19 - Gold Standard Abandoned (ratified June 5, 1933)

May 12 - Federal Emergency Relief Act

    Agricultural Adjustment Act

    Emergency Farm Mortgage Act

May 18 - Tennessee Valley Authority Act

May 27 - Truth-in-Securities Act

June 13 - Home Owner's Act

June 16 - National Industrial Recovery Act

    Glass-Steagall Banking Act

    Farm Credit Act

Within days of taking office, Henry Wallace and aides had crafted a farm bill to lay before FDR. The proposal was an about-face from the old McNary–Haugen Act which called for high tariffs and the dumping of surplus commodities on foreign markets. Wallace's idea would set up a domestic allotment program, which critics immediately labeled "planned scarcity."

The idea did not sail smoothly through the administrative maelstrom during those first Hundred Days, for a sizeable faction guided by George N. Peek was at odds with Rexford Guy Tugwell, Jerome Frank, and other advisors who had been persuaded to follow Henry Wallace.

Peek had played a major role in developing the two-price system urged by agricultural reformers in the 1920s, and he continued to give priority to domestic matters over all considerations of foreign trade. Peek saw Wallace and his believers as "internationalists" or "collectivists" who through acreage control were trying to regiment the American farmer.

Wallace and his group supported Secretary of State Cordell Hull's moves toward more free trade, and they opposed Peek's plans to raise farm income by disposing of agricultural surpluses abroad by means of dumping, subsidizing exports, and bilateral arrangements. Peek was a product of the Midwest with its corn/hog agriculture, its protectionist tariff views, and its less acute awareness of the importance of foreign markets. Hull, on the other hand, came from Tennessee and had grown up adopting views of most Southerners, long and consciously dependent on foreign markets for cotton and on foreign suppliers for industrial imports.

In May, 1933, when Wallace's proposal was enacted into the Agricultural Adjustment Act (AAA), President Roosevelt named Peek as the Agricultural Adjustment Administrator and placed the position under the authority of Cordell Hull, Secretary of State. Soon, however, rivalry between the Peek and Wallace factions was disruptive enough to threaten success of the new law. FDR, who found it difficult to dismiss anyone, tried to avoid taking sides and in December, 1933, he arranged to have Peek resign and accept leadership of a new organization designed "to coordinate all government relations to American foreign trade."[7]

With Peek's transfer and the AAA in place under the administration of the Secretary of Agriculture, Wallace had broader powers than any cabinet officer hitherto had enjoyed. He now had legal ways to meet the glut of farm products and their abysmally low prices. Wheat and corn at the time commanded a lower price per bushel than they had in colonial days three centuries earlier. The Triple A authorized the agriculture department through a system of county agents to reduce planting of staple commodities such as grain, cotton, tobacco, peanuts, and sugar; to plow under 10 million acres of the cotton already planted (for which owners were paid $200 million), and to reduce the breeding of pigs and cattle

The most painless program put in place under the AAA covered wheat growers. Growers of this crop tended to be less divided than other commodity groups; moreover, severe droughts in the Midwest reduced the surplus, so Wallace didn't have to worry much about wheat. His most perplexing problem was what to do about corn and hogs. He toyed with the idea of a long-range program to reduce corn by ten million acres and hogs by seven million head. But even with that, no real benefits would come to farmers in less than two years, and they needed help immediately.

Hog farmers themselves suggested a program to mandate slaughtering of pigs weighing less than one hundred pounds instead of feeding them until they reached two hundred pounds — the usual marketable weight. Under the plan, pigs would eat less corn, the total number of pigs would be reduced by five or six million, the price would rise, and edible portions of the little pigs could feed the hungry. Wallace fussed over the plan and delayed announcing it until August at the Chicago World's Fair.

No decision Wallace made as Secretary was more controversial than his program to kill six million baby pigs. Critics denounced him for committing "pig infanticide" or "pig birth control." He tried to counter such denouncements by saying, "Doubtless, it is just as inhumane to kill a big hog as a little one, but few people appreciate that."

The little pigs did not die in vain, however, for that fall the Federal Surplus Relief Corporation froze the pork surplus and distributed over 100 million pounds of it to families on relief. Moreover, tobacco growers who had received $43 million for their 1933 crop got $120 million in 1934. Comparable results were achieved in other farm products. The national farm income increased from $5.6 billion in 1932 to $8.7 billion in 1935.[8]

Destruction of food and paying growers not to produce rankled thousands of farmers whose lives were dedicated to larger yields and bringing more livestock to market, but in the overall view no other measure had ever been found to meet the recurrent problem of how to give farmers adequate returns for their labor.

During the first two administrations of Franklin Roosevelt, no department was more active than the Department of Agriculture under its energetic leader. On the day that AAA became law, Congress passed a companion measure — one developed and guided by Wallace — the Emergency Farm Mortgage Act. This Act halted farm foreclosures and provided federal refunding for existing mortgages.

Wallace threw his considerable support behind the Tennessee Valley Authority when it was proposed by George Norris, liberal senator from Nebraska. In 1936, Wallace helped engineer the Soil Conservation Act, which replaced the emergency AAA and provided for the reforestation of immense areas of marginal land throughout the country.

The Rural Electrification Administration, originally set up as a relief project, became an independent agency in 1936, and it, too, got an impetus from Henry Wallace as well as from George Norris. Probably no action by the Roosevelt administrations changed rural life more than did electrification.

When Wallace became Secretary of Agriculture in 1933, only one out of ten farms in America had electric power. The lighted "white way" of the city ended with its limit signs on a town's outskirts; farmers had been ignored. Nine out of ten farms in 1933 relied on horses, mules, and hand labor for power and kerosene lamps for light. Nearly twenty-four million of the thirty million citizens then working in agriculture had no bathtub or shower, lived with privies outside, carried water from wells or brooks, heated their homes by stoves, did their laundry and sometimes even bathed their children outdoors.

The Rural Electrification Administration got its money from Congress, and no federal program was ever more successful. By the end of 1941, REA had loaned $434 million to rural co-operative power plants, and the number of farms having electric light and power increased from 750,000 to 1,250,000. By 1950, ninety per cent of all farms in the U.S. were electrified.[9]

One of the last Acts passed hurriedly by the 73rd Congress before it adjourned in June, 1933, was the National Industrial Recovery Act — most often called simply the NRA — National Recovery Administration. The Act aimed to revive business and industrial activity and to reduce unemployment — the most visible sores of the depression.

Eight months after the seminal NRA had been passed by Congress, a National Recovery Board, primarily to enforce labor's rights for collective bargaining, was established. Business and industrial leaders saw such action as intrusions upon their rights, and eventually the issue reached the Supreme Court. Attorneys for the Administration insisted that grave economic conditions afflicting the nation had made labor codes and empowerment of the President necessary. The Court brushed aside such arguments and passed a unanimous ruling that in approving the National Recovery Act, Congress had exceeded its authority. "Extraordinary conditions do not create or enlarge constitutional powers," declared the nation's highest tribunal."[10]

An embittered FDR asserted in his next press conference that the Supreme Court's ruling had relegated the powers of the federal government to the "horse and buggy age." An imbroglio between New Dealers, the Judiciary, conservative critics, and public ensued and was an issue in the 1936 elections when Democrats swamped their opponents.

FDR with his dander up and lofted by his victory in winning a second term vowed to continue his fight with the Court. In collaboration with his Attorney General and young, liberal lawyers, FDR devised a plan giving the President power to appoint a federal judge for every one with ten years of service who had reached the age of seventy and had failed to retire. The scheme fueled further outrage, and even some stalwart Democrats began backing away. Henry Wallace was not one of them and stood by his chief throughout the fracas until it ended in 1937 when the plan finally was rejected by the Congress.

The world scene began darkening first in 1936 with the outbreak of civil war in Spain, soon followed by air attacks ordered by Italian Benito Mussolini, *Il Duce*, against defenseless Ethiopia. Also on the European continent, Nazi leader Adolf Hitler in violation of provisions in the Versailles Treaty moved into the Rhineland before annexing Austria and Czechoslovakia in quick succession. France and Britain stood aside, accepting Hitler's statement that he had no further territorial ambitions in Europe.

In America, President Roosevelt, well into his second term, and ever more confident in his own abilities, attempted to broker the situation by writing personal messages to Hitler and to Benito Mussolini asking them to pledge no military action against thirty-three European and Middle Eastern nations for at least ten years.

Henry Wallace asked the President not to send the messages and asserted, "There is danger that people in foreign lands and even some in this country will look upon your effort as being in the same category as delivering a sermon to a mad dog."

FDR failed to follow Wallace's warning, and his messages evoked humiliating responses. Hitler convened the Reichstag and amid laughter from his Nazi audience mocked the American president. Mussolini's reaction was even more insulting; he sneered that the request was "the result of infantile paralysis."[11]

Wallace's standing with FDR kept rising because of other measures introduced by him and his aides and was never higher than in the approach of 1940, an election year. From the inception of the New Deal in 1933 until after the election of 1936, Wallace either on his own promoted programs to strengthen American agriculture or followed FDR's leads. Problems of Europe and Asia seemed remote to American citizens, most of whom were struggling to eke out a living for their families. The nation was recovering from its greatest depression, and the domestic economy was still uppermost in the minds of most citizens.

At the time of his graduation from Iowa State College, Wallace had read a book describing a system of grain storage used by China as early as 54 B.C. One tenet in the book advanced the idea that when the price of grain was low, the ruling province should buy it at the normal price or higher than the market price, in order to profit farmers. When the grain price was high, the province should sell it at the normal price, lower than market price, in order to benefit consumers.

Wallace took the thesis to heart and coined his own term for it: the "ever normal granary." As Secretary of Agriculture the "ever normal granary" had almost been achieved, and in a nationally broadcast address Wallace reassured Americans that there was no cause for alarm over food shortages in this country:

> We are not at war, and we have an abundance of practically all kinds of food. We have reason to rejoice in the strength of our position. . . .
> Housewives don't know it yet, but they will soon find out that we have

in agriculture a mechanism [the ever normal granary] which in a measure does for agriculture what government insurance of banks does for banks.[12]

After war broke out in Europe in early fall of 1939, FDR did all he could to help the British — lending (without congressional approval) fifty destroyers to Britain, arming American merchant marine ships, increasing expenditures for military build-ups, and adding complicated amendments to neutrality legislation. In 1940, under his urging, Congress enacted the nation's first peacetime draft. Nine hundred thousand selectees were taken each year, and in August, 1941, the promised one-year enlistment period was extended to eighteen months.

Through loyalty and his own beliefs, Wallace endorsed the moves, and began to speak out more about world trade policies, food, and war — predictable struggles between the "have" and "have-not" nations. Wallace didn't equivocate about Hitler's assertion of Aryan superiority, calling the idea absurd and contrary to what every true scientist knew.

On the political front, FDR was coy about running for a third term and would not publicly state his intentions; his strategy was to have the Democratic Nominating Convention announce it. He told confidantes that *if* he were to be chosen at the convention he would be a candidate because he "had no more right to refuse serving his nation than did soldiers or sailors" who already were doing that. Behind the scenes, he sent Harry Hopkins to set up headquarters in Chicago where, in July 1940 delegates would meet, and he summoned Samuel Rosenman to the White House in order to prepare an acceptance speech.

Henry Wallace had been convinced as early as 1939 that Roosevelt wanted to run for a third term. In Wallace's view, not only did FDR want to run but events in Europe had made his run mandatory. In a 1939 press conference held in San Francisco, the Secretary said,

> Mr. Roosevelt's background seems to equip him with exceptional qualifications as a helmsman to steer the country through both foreign and domestic troubles to a safe harbor.[13]

Democrats began their national convention on July 15, 1940, and according to one newspaper reporter, delegates arrived with all "the enthusiasm of a chain gang." Everyone had come knowing that Franklin Roosevelt was to be re-nominated; the only real question was over who would be his running mate. There were several in the dug-out hoping to be called. Vice President Garner was available, but he had declared his opposition to a third term for FDR. Labor leader John L. Lewis acidly put down the vice president by commenting that Garner "was a labor-baiting, poker-playing, whiskey-drinking, evil old man." And finally, Garner's acknowledged conservatism made him unacceptable to liberals in the party.

Others were in the running. There was Jimmy Byrnes, who liked to be called the "Assistant President," but he was an anathema to organized labor. James Farley, genial Irishman, was in the wings and would have liked the job, but his Catholicism and lack of knowledge about economics and foreign affairs was dumbfounding. William O. Douglas, head of the Securities and Exchange Commission, and Attorney General Robert H. Jackson had the presidential urge but little professional political support. Paul V. McNutt, former governor of Indiana, hoped to be chosen, but he failed to get the nod from FDR.

The President's first choice for a running mate that year had been Harry Hopkins, but the precarious health of this close advisor as well as his marital and political difficulties were certain to drive away many voters. Cordell Hull might have been a good choice, for he had been faithful to FDR and held similar views insofar as foreign trade policies were involved. Hull's health, however, was not strong, and he remained silent about any political goals. Farther down the list of possible candidates was Henry Wallace.

After Hopkins had been taken out of the race, an insider Washington clique led by Harold Ickes and Tommy "the Cork" Corcoran pressured Wallace to join them. The two leaders were aware their boss was weighing the advantages of having Wallace on the campaign ticket. Wallace was a genuine New Dealer, an internationalist, a loyalist on the Supreme Court issue and on the third term decision. He was in vigorous health, a Protestant, and had an imposing agricultural constituency. When Farley and others in his circle of advisors raised questions about Wallace, FDR brushed them aside. He would have Wallace or he would refuse to run.

In that summer of 1940, across America sympathy for embattled Britain was mounting, and in July when Republicans met in Philadelphia for their nominating convention, three stalwarts were seeking top place on the ticket: Senator Robert Taft of Ohio, Senator Arthur Vandenberg of Michigan, and Thomas E. Dewey, the vigorous, gang-busting Attorney General from Manhattan.

The three leaders were shunted aside, however, when delegates began a stampede for a black horse candidate, Wendell L. Willkie.

Throughout the convention hall came gusty shouts: "We Want Willkie! We Want Willkie!" Nevertheless, it took six ballots before the former Hoosier was chosen as the party's nominee.

Willkie, with his law degree from Indiana University, was a corporation lawyer, and had served as an officer in World War I. In 1929 — the year the crash began — he was named legal counsel for the New York-based Common Wealth and Southern Corporation, the nation's largest electric utility holding company. The Tennessee Valley Authority brought the government into direct competition with private companies, including Common Wealth and Southern. The confrontation forced Willkie to become an active critic of TVA as well as other New Deal agencies.

No issue during the campaign that summer and fall fired the public as much as the threat of being dragged into the European war. Willkie was not an isolationist, and his candidacy buoyed Republican hopes, but he was facing an incumbent president at the height of his power and prestige and also the most adroit politician the country had ever known.

As in most campaigns, there were dirty tricks. Republicans reiterated their calumnies against FDR, and Democrats retaliated by reminding voters that in earlier years Willkie had been a registered Democrat. Blue collar toughs booed Willkie, and once standing by his side on the speaker's platform, his wife was hit by an egg. The Democratic candidate for the presidency, Henry Wallace, fired some of the most vicious allegations, charging that Willkie was the Nazis' first choice.

Late in the campaign, Republicans discovered letters Wallace had written to a Russian mystic named Nicholas Roerich. In the letters, Wallace addressed Roerich as "Dear Guru," and signed his own name as "G" for Galahad, the title Roerich had bestowed on him as a member of the faith. In his correspondence, Wallace assured Roerich that there would be "a breaking of the New Day," when the people of "Northern Shambella" (a Buddhist term roughly equivalent to the kingdom of heaven) would establish an era of peace and plenty.[14]

Upon learning the letters had been discovered, Democratic politicos were extremely fearful that if they became public and Wallace's eccentricities exposed, the entire ticket would be in jeopardy.

Republicans did threaten to reveal the letters but put the idea aside when Democrats warned they would get even by giving out information about Willkie's rumored extramarital affair with writer Irita Van Doren.[15] The twin threats worked, and neither scandal surfaced until well after the election had been decided.

That November, FDR received 449 electoral votes compared with Willkie's 82, and Secretary of Agriculture Henry Wallace was elevated to the Vice Presidency, only a heartbeat away from the nation's highest elective office.

On January 20, 1941, a cold wintry day, shortly after the noon hour, Wallace became the country's thirty-third vice president. He gave no speech at his inauguration, saying only "I do" in vowing to accept his new job. His first act as vice president was to get rid of the wet bar his predecessor had installed in the formal office of the vice president. Using it to fuel intimacy, John Garner had built many "bottled-in-bond" friendships and political allegiances. The incoming vice president told reporters he hoped those coming into the office to see him would accept "good cigars" in lieu of whisky.

He also said he intended to give no speeches, but that intent was cast aside the next month when he addressed listeners at the National Farm Institute in Des Moines. In his talk there, Wallace called for military preparedness and attempted to build support for his chief's plan to provide Britain with military supplies through Lend Lease — a proposal then being debated in Congress and across the country.

The Constitution gives the Vice President the duty of presiding over the U.S. Senate, where he can vote only to break a tie. Fulfilling his duties in the Senate was a bore for Wallace. He thought the debates — often more than seven hours per day — were tedious and repetitive. His interest in the workings of Congress was at best only modest, and he didn't indulge in the gregarious, back-slapping camaraderie of many politicians. In the Vice Presidency, Wallace was less busy than he had been in the two previous decades.

The hiatus ended in August 1941, when President Roosevelt issued an Executive Order creating the Supply Priorities and Allocation Board (SPAB) and named Wallace as its chairman. In that position, Wallace became one of the most powerful men in Washington; his strength derived from the fact the President wanted him. He was FDR's man, and he intended to do exactly what his superior wanted. Wallace quickly issued a public statement setting out goals for the SPAB:

> Our general policy is simple. Production shall be stimulated and organized to the limit of the nation's resources. Every available man and machine must be employed either on direct defense requirements or on work essential to the civilian economy. Along this road lies protection of our freedom and of the basic economy necessary to the maintenance of that freedom.[16]

Not until 1940 had Wallace paid much attention to foreign policies, concentrating instead on domestic matters. In 1940, however, as FDR's running mate, he spoke out more frequently in favor of liberal trade policies, revisions of neutrality, and rearmament programs, thus supporting positions of the administration; and after America entered the war, he increasingly stressed the lack of morality found in dictatorships.

No member was more loyal to the administration than Vice President Wallace, yet as the election year of 1944 approached FDR had developed reservations about re-naming Wallace as a running mate. Wallace was a liberal, all right, but he was irregular and had unusual habits that alienated large segments of voters — voters FDR always weighed very carefully. The matter of the vice presidency must have been of little importance to him anyway, for there is no evidence he ever gave much thought to a successor; certainly he never attempted in any way to orient his vice presidents to the duties and problems in the oval office.

Leading figures who some pundits thought might be chosen for the vice presidential slot in 1944 were Supreme Court Justice William O. Douglas, War Mobilization Director James Byrnes, and Senator Alben Barkely of Kentucky. Vice President Wallace was far down on the list of candidates.

Admittedly, Wallace was admired by most fervent New Dealers, but he was looked down upon by party bosses and lampooned by Southern Democrats as a dreamer who "wanted a quart of milk for every Hottentot." Within the Democratic Party, a powerful group consisting of National Chairman Robert Hannegan, Postmaster General Frank Walker, millionaire Edwin Pauley, and Mayor Ed Kelley of Chicago, was determined that Henry Wallace should never be in a position to become President of the United States. This group, abetted by a few others, was able to convince the President that he should choose another running mate.

The dissenting group went through a list of candidates before deciding on Senator Harry Truman of Missouri. Truman's name brought virtually no opposition. His voting record had been consistently New Deal; he was from a border state and was popular with that exclusive and influential body — the U.S. Senate, and he had won strong newspaper support for his work as chairman of the important Senate War Investigating Committee. And of utmost importance, he was acceptable to the President.

Wallace though was not a person who gave up easily and at his urging, President Roosevelt agreed to write a letter stating that if he were a delegate at the Democratic convention he personally would vote for Henry Wallace.

As conventioneers began assembling, National Democratic Chairman Robert Hannegan alarmed over indecisions of delegates regarding Byrnes, Douglas, Barkely, and Wallace immediately telephoned President Roosevelt who was preparing for a trip to San Diego. Hannegan was able to secure from FDR a letter stating, "You have written me about Bill Douglas and Harry Truman. I would, of course, be very glad to run with either of them and believe that either of them would bring real strength to the ticket."[17]

Hannegan and his colleagues were not pleased with the inclusion of Douglas's name, and in the re-typing of the letter the two names were reversed. Thus Truman was not yet the unequivocal choice, but it was clear that Wallace was no longer Roosevelt's preference.

America had been at war for three years when the election of 1944 came about, and voters had no wish to change leaders. The Roosevelt–Truman ticket won easily with 25,602,205 popular votes compared with the 22,006,278 for Republican opponents. The electoral count was even more impressive with Democrats capturing 81.36% (432 votes) to 18.64% (99 votes) for the rival Dewey–Bricker slate.

Understandably embittered over having been "dumped" by FDR, Wallace nevertheless withheld his chagrin, only expressing it years later in memoirs and oral histories. Yet soon after the election he confronted FDR to seek an explanation. Roosevelt, as was his custom, diverted the conversation into parallels from the Wilson administration and tried to assure Wallace that he and his talents were still highly regarded. To show that he had lost none of his standing, FDR offered Wallace any cabinet position he wanted except Secretary of State. Cordell Hull was too valuable in that spot to be replaced. Wallace opted for Secretary of Commerce and was appointed to the post in January when FDR began his fourth term.

Wallace hardly had time to become ensconced in the new office before President Roosevelt died. Incoming President Truman opted to keep Wallace in his cabinet position, however; the two men respected each other and even had walked into the nominating convention together nine months earlier.

The urgency forced on President Truman immediately after April 12, 1945, did not permit the careful screening and examination a more normal transfer of administrations would have offered, and because Roosevelt had done nothing to help a successor, Truman inherited FDR's cabinet.

America felt they had been at war long enough, and most citizens were looking outwardly toward it and international matters more than inwardly toward domestic policies. Yet foreign policy was the field in which Truman was most untested.

Throughout his first year in the presidency, Truman's liberalism was still an uncertain quality; known liberals around him were in the minority. Chester Bowles, Harold Ickes, Henry Morgenthau, Jr., and Fred Vinson had departed. A small group in Truman's confidence included newer figures such as Charles S. Murphy, Oscar Ewing, Oscar Chapman, and later Leon Keyserling. This decidedly liberal wing was led by Clark Clifford, whom Truman in late 1946 had appointed as Special Counsel to the President.

Clifford recognized the schism surrounding President Truman and once gave his account of the struggle between the two blocs vying for Truman's backing in 1946:

Naturally, we were up against tough competition. Most of the Cabinet and the congressional leaders were urging Mr. Truman to go slow, to veer a little closer to the conservative line. They held the image of Bob Taft before him like a ghost. It was an increasing struggle those years, and it got to the point where no quarter was asked, and none was given.[18]

By far the most vexing problems facing President Truman were those involving American–Soviet relations. War time cooperation had begun unraveling even before the ink had dried on accords signed at Yalta. None of the signatories interpreted the loosely worded agreements in the same way. Churchill began to argue for more Western influence; Stalin advocated less. FDR's strategy had been to act as a mediator between the British and the Russians and to postpone integral decisions that might disrupt the alliance.

Wallace, although not as close to Truman as Clifford and some of the other liberals, nevertheless was a Truman supporter and loyal Cabinet member as Secretary of Commerce. The fiasco which ruptured their harmony came in September of 1945.

Secretary of State James Byrnes was in Paris for another meeting of the moribund Council of Foreign Ministers, and back in America Henry Wallace was scheduled to give a talk in New York City. Relations between the Soviets and America were deteriorating, and the rally at which Wallace was to speak was billed with the purpose of restoring earlier friendships.

Wallace came to the White House and in conference with President Truman told him about some of the ideas he meant to address. As the two talked, Truman thumbed through the manuscript. No problems were raised, and President Truman shifted the conversation to the forthcoming political elections. Truman told Wallace he hoped he would continue trying to garner liberal voting blocs for Democratic candidates, adding that he thought the speech ought to boost chances for Herbert Lehman and James Meade, candidates in New York for governor and senator respectively.

Wallace left the president's office encouraged by what he thought was complete support, and as a result he inserted a new sentence in the speech: "When President Truman read these words he said they represented the policy of this administration." The following Saturday when Wallace spoke in Madison Square Garden, there was considerable clamor and confusion. He was interrupted frequently by applause and occasional booing. The sentences immediately preceding the one in which he stated he had gained the president's approval read: "In this connection, I want one thing clearly understood. I am neither anti-British nor pro-British — neither anti-Russian nor pro-Russian." At another point in the talk, Wallace asserted that China should remain free from any sphere of influence, and then he ad-libbed, "Mr. Truman read that particular sentence, and he approved it."

From the references to President Truman, it was not clear to all listeners whether Wallace was saying the President had approved particular sentences or the entire speech, but after conclusion of his talk Wallace contended to reporters that President Truman had gone over the speech page by page.

Taken in its entire context, there is no doubt Wallace's speech carried severe criticism of Soviet actions, but it also criticized Western powers for failing to recognize Russian's innate suspicions of the capitalist world.

The contretemps had been muddied more by a presidential press conference two days before the speech was delivered, and when one of several reporters who had been given advance copies of Wallace's intended speech asked if the line about representing the policy of the administration was accurate. President Truman breezily replied that the statement was correct. The reporter persisted and asked, "My question is, does that apply to that paragraph or to the whole speech?" That President answered, "I approved the whole speech."

The press conference had hardly ended before it was evident Truman had blundered. The State Department phoned the President's office to ask if such an answer really had been given. The Navy Department was upset because it felt the statement swept the ground out from under Secretary of State James Byrnes, then meeting with the Russians in Paris. Indeed, Byrnes cabled his chief threatening to resign unless Wallace could be kept from making more criticisms of foreign policy. Senator Arthur Vandenberg, Republican bipartisan leader who had accompanied Byrnes to the Paris meetings, issued an indignant, "I can cooperate with only one Secretary of State at a time."

For a week reverberations from the speech and press conferences occupied most of President Truman's attention; he called reporters into his office and tried to repair the damage by handing out a written statement including the sentence: "There has been no change in the established foreign policy of our government."[19]

By September 19th, President Truman had had enough; he wrote out a letter in longhand and sent it to Wallace asking for his resignation. The die was cast, and Wallace obligingly responded the day he received the request.

American–Soviet relations slid downhill faster. The toughening stance toward Russia was not a change that could be traced to a single event or date. Nor is it likely that the change came from a carefully planned strategy of the Truman administration. Rather it was a policy that grew on a week-by-week basis as military urgencies lessened and new arrangements had to be made.

On February 9, 1946, Russian Premier Josef Stalin made a speech in Moscow, and in it was a blunt rejection of any chance of an enduring peace with the West. Stalin blamed World War II on capitalism, and declared that as long as capitalists controlled any part of the world, there could be no hope for peace. He insisted the Soviet Union must rearm, and he called for trebling his country's production of iron, steel, and coal in order to guarantee Russia against any eventuality.

A few days after that blast, George F. Kennan, the U.S. *Chargé d'Affaires* in Moscow, returned to America bringing with him a long report which when published became known as "The Sources of Soviet Conduct." The report signed by "X" described the Kremlin's neurotic view of world history stemming from its traditional sense of insecurity. Stripped of their Marxist justifications, Kennan wrote that Soviet leaders would stand before history as merely the last of a long succession of cruel and wasteful Russian rulers who forced their country into military ventures taken to guarantee external security for their own internally weak regimes.

Some Western historians put great emphasis upon this report as being one of the significant documents helping form the "Truman Doctrine," i.e., stricter bargaining with the Soviets — a policy commonly called "getting tough with Russia." George Elsey, map room coordinator for Roosevelt and a prime speech writer for President Truman, echoed Margaret Truman's assertions that Kennan's report did not strike anyone in her father's administration as telling anything not already known, and Elsey said that whatever shock value the report contained was only on those wishful thinkers who bought the gospel preached by Henry Wallace that the trouble with Russia was all America's fault.[20]

In March 1946, Winston Churchill came to the U.S. and with President Truman sitting on the platform beside him, Britain's war leader and hero described Soviet aggrandizements and declared, "From Stettin in the Baltic to Trieste in the Adriatic an *iron curtain* has descended across the Continent." A year later on March 15, 1947, President Truman asked Congress for food and military aid to embattled Greece and Turkey, then under aggressions by Russian infiltrators.

No longer in office, Wallace was free to enjoy the huge profits being reaped by Pioneer Hi-Bred Seed Corn, yet he continued his abstemious living habits. While he had been faithful to President Roosevelt, he had never been much of a Party man — either as Republican or Democrat. Political parties to him were merely baggage necessary to get things done. He traveled more, and wherever he went he spoke out for liberal foreign trade policies.

An unabashed idealist, his themes were built around the sublime character of the human spirit and included appeals for cooperation rather than rivalry among nations. Such sentiments necessarily clashed with the "Get Tough With Russia" measures being adopted by the American Congress, so inevitably Wallace was seen as a roving critic of the Truman administration, a maverick abandoned by both major political parties.

The war had been over for a year and a half, but Wallace was appalled by the devastation he saw throughout Europe. His heart went out for the poor, the hungry, and the homeless. He had been a controversial figure throughout the New Deal, and wherever he went reporters sought him out, seeking reasons for his pilgrimage and opinions for what he had seen. In Paris during April 1947, he was interviewed by reporters and gave off-the-cuff answers to their probing questions. One particular response — a reference to Russia, once an ally and now considered a threat by the Truman administration — would resurface to plague his later years. Wallace himself explained it best in a letter to this author:[21]

FARVUE FARM   SOUTH SALEM   NEW YORK

Aug. 31, 1954.

Dear Prof. Underhill,

In cleaning up my desk I ran across your letter of Aug. 17 and noted some points which I had overlooked. In someways the most important talk I gave in the spring of 1947 was to about 200 members of the French Chamber of Deputies. It was extemporaneous and I do not think was taken down. It was reported somewhat inaccurately in the Paris edition of the New York Herald Tribune about April 25, 1945. My thesis was that if Russia insisted on taking $10 billion dollars in reparations out of Germany she would make a cess pool out of Germany. Therefore I proposed that the US should make available over a period 5 or 10 years a total of $50 billion with the distribution to be made on the basis of war damage. Someone asked me how much this would mean for Russia. I said I did not know but would presume that the extent of her damage might entitle her on a pro rata basis to perhaps $10 or $20 billion worth. Naturally this stole the headlines and noone paid any attention to the broad outline of my argument. A little late the Marshall plan was born which in the first instance followed my approach to some degree. Unfortunately Russia turned it down. From then on it became increasingly clear that Russia wanted the cold war. Some day I suppose we shall know the full story of why the Marshall plan was turned down by Russia.

Sincerely yours,

H A Wallace

Note that in the speech he cites, his proposal of some $850 billion in aid to Europe foreshadowed the Marshall Plan which was announced a short time afterward. (Mr. Wallace in this letter must have confused the years of 1946 and 1947.)

Great Britain, having lost so many export markets, was in serious financial straits in 1947, and at the same time the economies of France, Italy, and other countries in Europe were teetering on the verge of collapse with prospects of communist takeovers.

The pot had begun boiling even before the war in Europe ended. In September, 1944, when President Roosevelt and Prime Minister Churchill met for their conference in Quebec, no issue was more divisive than treatment of postwar Germany. At that time, Allied victories were mounting; ground forces had penetrated Belgium and seized bridges over rivers and canal lines. Allied diplomats agreed that the German army would have to be destroyed and that Nazi leaders should be severely punished. But what about the German Government itself? What kind of an economy should it establish?

In American councils, two of President Roosevelt's major advisors offered differing plans. Secretary of the Treasury Henry Morgenthau submitted a draconian scheme which meant to turn Germany into an agricultural nation, obliterating the huge industrial resources of the Ruhr Valley. Secretary of War Henry Stinson adamantly opposed the idea of destroying such a "great gift of nature."

President Roosevelt listened to both advisors but equivocated, leading each of the two Cabinet officers to believe his idea was going to be the one followed.

Ink had not dried on surrender documents before old rivalries and fears again rose to the surface. Wartime friendliness and cooperation were replaced by suspicion and competition. Yes, Germany was a militaristic nation, but the Soviet Union also was a threat. The prevailing opinion in America was a "Get Tough With Russia" policy. And by the summer of 1947, Churchill with President Harry Truman on the platform beside him in Fulton, Missouri, had delivered an eloquent warning of an *Iron Curtain* which had descended over Europe. This was the atmosphere when General George C. Marshall, Secretary of State after Hull's retirement, announced in a speech at Harvard University a plan to help restore the shattered economies.

A generous gesture from President Truman encouraged the press to name the European Recovery Administration after the wartime hero, and soon it became the Marshall Plan, essentially following the outline described by Wallace a month earlier. Of course, Wallace was given no credit for having mentioned it. The nub of the Marshall Plan was that European countries which needed help should make their own reconstruction plans, not so much for immediate relief as "to permit the emergence of political and social conditions in which free institutions can exist." The European nations must plan for themselves.

Marshall's idea was seized upon immediately by every European country not under communist control. Russia was offered its benefits but turned down the proposal and encouraged her satellites to do the same; perhaps the reason for the turndown was fear that the plan would destroy Stalin's hopes for a capitalist collapse.

After resigning from his cabinet position, Wallace became publisher of the weekly *New Republic*, an organ in which he could advance his opinions through occasional essays. Soon after inception of the Marshall Plan, Wallace endorsed it, writing in the *New Republic* that the doctrine looked toward an overall program he himself had been advocating for "some time." Only later when aspects of the Plan showed evidence of its being a factor in the Cold War did his enthusiasm for it begin to flag.

During that summer and fall of 1947 Wallace was pulled in many directions. Russia pressured its satellites, especially Poland and Czechoslovakia, to stay out of the Marshall Plan, and from Moscow the Soviets launched propaganda which was like pouring gasoline onto smoldering embers of American fears of an international conspiracy.

Wallace argued that Russia's rejection came from the rigidity of the Truman Doctrine — embodiment of the "Get Tough with Russia" concept. He suggested putting ERA under the auspices of the United Nations, but that idea fell on deaf ears.

Some liberals indeed were distraught over the Truman Doctrine but announced they would not leave the Democratic Party. Others, looking for a different champion, began courting Wallace anew. The chairman of a group called Progressive Citizens of America (PCA) invited him to speak at several rallies scattered across the U.S., and it was through this agency and encouragement from Michael Straight, editor of the *New Republic*, that in October 1947, Wallace went on a tour of the Near East with the express purpose of visiting the newly created State of Israel.

Reporters followed him seeking comments on what he found in the Jewish or Arab communities, but he dodged such inquiries and concentrated on advising farmers in both regions on agricultural problems. His only public announcement during these two weeks abroad was not about Palestine-Arab strife but about Red-baiting practices going on at home. The House Un-American Activities was conducting a celebrated series of hearings on communism in Hollywood — hearings which eventually sent ten screenwriters and directors to jail.

Two days before the year of 1947 ended and nearly six months before active campaigning for the presidency would get underway, Wallace gave a pivotal speech over the Mutual Broadcasting System from a Chicago station. He expressed his ideals for a lasting peace — the kind of international harmony that "would usher in the century of the common man." Then he tried to rebut the argument that casting a vote for any third party would be wasting it; such votes had won for Thomas Jefferson a triumph over the Federalists, and independent people won it again when the Republican Party was organized in Lincoln's time. Next he addressed the Marshall Plan, stating again that he was as committed as ever to humanitarian assistance to Europe, but he decried the use of that aid as a factor in any "getting tough with Russia" doctrine. Aware of the need to address charges that he was a pawn for communism, he declared,

> I am against any kind of imperialism or expansionism whether sponsored by Britain, Russia, or the United States, and I call upon Russia as well as the United States to look at all our differences objectively and free from the prejudice which hate mongers have engendered on both side.[22]

The Progressive Citizens of America claimed to have 100,000 members in 1948, but its treasury was not even close to the amount necessary for a national campaign. And aside from money matters were the difficulties of getting a third party on the ballot in numerous states; some states set very early deadlines for formation of such groups, and others demanded signed petitions from large numbers of the state's residents. Disturbingly, too, was a proposal being weighed in Congress to ban from the ballot all "un-American parties . . . directly or indirectly affiliated . . . with the Communist Party."

Only fervent Red-baiters thought Wallace an outright Communist, but millions accepted charges that he was a "dupe" or "fellow traveler" being used by Soviet agents. Indeed, Communist leaders in America, namely William Z. Foster, head of the Communist Party in the U.S., and Eugene Dennis, its general secretary in the U.S., were quick to exaggerate their roles in Wallace's 1948 presidential run.

In the fourth week of July, 1948, more than 3200 rambunctious delegates met in Philadelphia, and taking heed of the country's history formed a new party, to be called the Progressive Party. Wallace was the Party's overwhelming choice as its presidential nominee. Twice before, third-party candidates had run under the Progressive banner; thus Henry Wallace would follow in the footsteps of Theodore Roosevelt and Robert La Follette.

As weeks passed, Wallace came to see the Marshall Plan as an element in the Cold War, so his attempted explanations that he favored economic help irrespective of political alliances aroused only more suspicions. His liberal views regarding rehabilitation of all devastated countries were overlooked. Added to his difficulties came revelations of his letters and naïve association with the questionable Nicholas Roerich twenty years earlier.

On several occasions, Wallace was pestered with questions: "What were the details of his association with Roerich?" "Would he repudiate some of the reported statements?" "Did he actually write the letters?" He refused to respond to such questions and muddied the water more by asserting he wouldn't answer "because it is not important."

Nor would echoes of communism fade away. Those charges alone would be enough to doom his candidacy, for no matter how hard he tried to present his conception of world peace as a result of cooperation rather than antagonism among nations, he couldn't escape the appearance of defending the Soviets. His plight worsened as known communists in America began voicing their support of his candidacy.

Strapped for funds, the Progressive Party leadership planned a series of fund-raising events for different parts of the nation. The obstreperous gatherings followed a pattern. J. Raymond Walsh, head of the PCA's New York chapter or a similar bigwig, would welcome all attendees, expound the high goals of the new party, and then invite down to the stage three to five major benefactors — ones who had donated $10,000 or more. Each would be introduced and thanked while an overhead spotlight focused on him or her. To add variety, a folk singer, usually Pete Seeger or Michael Loring, would sing their trademark songs with lyrics modified to fit the Progressive cause. Often a labor leader would be presented; in a meeting held in Chicago's public arena the leader was a Detroit union man who sang about "Who's going to investigate the man who investigates me?" It was a snide swipe at the House Investigating Committee.

Then in another pitch for funds, donors of $5,000 or more would be asked to stand by their seats while an overhead spotlight focused on each as from the stage the emcee read their names and business positions. Next, Paul Robeson, already an avowed communist, would be introduced and make a few remarks before, with his magnificent voice, he launched into *Ole Man River*, with "we just keep *fighting*" rather than just "keep *rolling* along."

After Robeson, Walsh or whoever was the emcee would ask for $1000 donations and would promise that such givers would be duly noted in brochures and leaflets put out by the party. In a final appeal, Walsh would say that he would like to look out over the vast audience and see "nothing but a sea of greenbacks," so each attendee was asked to take out $10, $5, or $1 — whatever he had in his wallet — stand and wave it so ushers could pick it up.

If a person remained sitting, a merciless spotlight would play on him until he relented and stood with the others.[23]

Then at last — nearly three hours after the meeting had been officially opened — Henry Wallace would be introduced. The crowd would explode with applause while Wallace would bow and box around the stage until the clamor began to subside. In his speech he would indict the "get-tough policy," cite need for compassion and understanding of the war's terrible devastation, and the necessity of a "brotherhood of man," which often included scriptural and biblical references.

He could not escape the taint of communism; it followed him wherever he went. Communists could not distribute their literature inside the halls where he spoke, but before people went in they usually were accosted by American communists scattered outside who would buttonhole them and thrust copies of *The Daily Worker* or other communist pamphlets into their hands.

Throughout the campaign, Wallace was cheered, booed, hissed, and the target for eggs, tomatoes, and other garbage. In nearly every such instance, his response was restrained and forgiving. He told aides that such hostility arose because people did not have enough to eat.

Despite Wallace's fund-raising events, the enthusiasm of his followers, and the sublimity of his messages as well as his energy in expressing them, the odds were against him. Thousands of rank-and-file liberals feared Dewey and the Republican Congress, and in result flocked in droves to elect President Truman.

That November, 1948, Truman garnered more than 24 million popular votes and 303 electoral votes compared with his Republican rival, Thomas Dewey's 22 million popular and 189 electoral college votes. Dixiecrat Strom Thurmond ran third with 1,169,032 popular votes, and Wallace came in last with 1,157,063 popular votes and no electoral college votes.

Although overwhelmed by the vote count, some observers believed Henry Wallace had made his mark, if not on foreign affairs, certainly upon domestic matters. President Truman and the Democratic Party grew increasingly liberal toward labor and agricultural problems, adopting relief measures for workers, farmers, and home-owners.

Wallace was not yet done with politics; he gave more than thirty speeches in the first seven months of 1949. For two years, he traveled the country preaching a gospel for international cooperation rather than competition. In testimony before congressional committees he criticized the "Cold War" aspects of the European Recovery Administration and vigorously opposed the very idea of the North Atlantic Treaty Organization (NATO). Increasingly, he paired criticisms of U.S. policies with his indictments of the Communists, insisting that Soviet suppression of civil liberties in the satellite nations must stop. His views led to alienation from much of the Progressive party, and the final break came in the summer of 1950 when North Korean troops in Russian-made tanks crossed the thirty-eighth parallel, the artificial lines separating Korea's north and south regions.

There was a series of letters and telephone calls from Wallace to Progressive party leaders in which he criticized Russia in the attack on South Korea. If the Soviets had not been the initiators, certainly they could easily have stopped the attack or prevented it from taking place. In any event, if America was in a war sanctioned by the United Nations, Wallace declared himself unequivocally on the side of his country. He failed in his attempts to get party leaders to join him in condemnation of Soviet actions, and in August, 1950, he formally resigned from the Progressive Party.

With that action, he vowed he was going to stay out of politics, but no figure as popular, divisive, and controversial as he could retire in seclusion. Moreover, the early 1950s were years when fears of communist conspiracies were used to keep citizens on edge. Some cases of spying indeed were exposed, and in sensational testimony before congressional committees, professional ex-Communist witnesses and FBI's counter spies smeared Wallace as an agent or at least a naïve and willing Communist dupe. It took nearly a decade before the grasp of anti-Communist hysteria relaxed its hold on America.

By this time, Henry Wallace had severed ties with Progressives, Democrats, and Republican politicians and was managing his farm in New York State where he raised golf ball-sized strawberries, mammoth hydroponic tomatoes, Chinese cabbages, gigantic gladioli, and, of course, rows upon rows of experimental corn. Even beyond his experiments with vegetables were his chickens — at one time numbering more than 15,000. Ever the scientist, he was continually involved in the processes of inbreeding and crossbreeding chicken, culling out undesirable strains and promulgating desirable characteristics.

In 1964, Wallace began to show the first symptoms of the disease which would claim his life. He was in Central America and climbing a pyramid in Guatemala when his left foot began to drag. Back home his muscular control worsened, and in November he went to the Mayo Clinic in Rochester, Minnesota, where he was diagnosed as suffering from amyotrophic lateral sclerosis (ALS), a rare neuromuscular degenerative disease. With his scientific bent he soon learned that no cure for ALS had been found (and still has not) and that the disease was fatal.

Yet Wallace did not give up. He exchanged letters with President Lyndon Johnson advancing ideas for stemming the alarming flight of farmers from the land and advocated a program wherein farmers could find enough part-time work in nearby towns to sustain themselves while on the farm.

Near the end of October 1965, Wallace was bedridden and was returned to his farm at Farvue, New York. His condition worsened, and three weeks later he was transferred to Danbury Hospital where at 11:15 A.M. on November 18, 1965, with his wife Ilo and his sister Mary in the room with him, he breathed his last.

Henry Wallace was a paradox — a politician and economist who tried to curtail food production in order to control market prices, yet as a scientist he promoted hybridization of basic crops, particularly corn, to produce yields which doubled or even tripled former ones. A vegetarian, he came from a state which bred more hogs than any other, and as a registered Republican he served thirteen years as a cabinet member in a decidedly Democratic administration.

Made wealthy by commercialization of hybrid corn, he was unpretentious and regarded as a common man. A farmer and scientist by nature and training, he lived most of his adult life among political chiefs and business leaders. He formed Pioneer Hi-Bred Seed Corn Company — one of the nation's most prominent corporations — which revolutionized crop farming in America.

Henry A. Wallace will be remembered by some as a maverick, but he was foremost among leaders who dared to sever party affiliations and follow his conscience wherever it led him — a true rebel.

Chronology of Henry Agard Wallace

Born . . . October 7, 1888, on a farm near Orient, Iowa.

Parents . . . Henry Cantwell Wallace and May (née Broadhead) Wallace

West High School in Des Moines . . . 1902–1906

Graduated from Iowa State College of Agricultural and Mechanic Arts . . . June, 1910

Associate Editor, Wallace's Farmer . . . 1910–1924

Married Ilo Browne . . . May 20, 1914

Founded Hi-Bred Pioneer Seed Corn Co. . . . May, 1926

Secretary of Agriculture . . . 1933–1940

Congress Passed Emergency Agriculture Adjustment Act. . . May 12, 1933

Vice President of the U.S. 1940–1944

Appointed Secretary of Commerce . . . 1945

Resigned from Secretary of Commerce . . . 1946

Editor of *New Republic Magazine* . . . 1946–1948

Presidential Candidate of Progressive Party . . . 1948

Death . . . November 18, 1965

ENDNOTES

Chapter 1. Ignatius Donnelly: Apostle of Protest

[1] Donnelly, Ignatius. *Atlantis: the Antediluvian World*. New York: Harper & Brothers, 1882.

[2] The Donnelly Papers located in the Minnesota Historical Society, St. Paul. The collection totals 95 boxes, and this quotation is in a Scrapbook, showing galley proof of a speech delivered at Red Wing, MN, July 4, 1871. Hereinafter these Papers will be referred to as Donnelly Papers.

[3] Holbrook, Stewart. *Lost Men of American History*. New York: The Macmillan Co., 1946. Pp. 268-69.

[4] Michael Kazin. *A Godly Hero: The Life of William Jennings Bryan*. New York: Alfred A. Knopf, 2006, pp. 56-57.

[5] Johnson, Gerald W. *The Lunatic Fringe*. New York: J. B. Lippincott Company, 1957, pp. 227-229.

[6] George, Henry. *Progress and Poverty*. 75th Anniversary ed. New York: Robert Schalkenbach Foundation, 1954, p. 343.

[7] Holbrook, *op. cit.*, p. 281.

[8] Rough draft of an editorial found in the Donnelly Papers. These Papers consist of 95 boxes and are held in the Minnesota Historical Society, St. Paul, Mn.

[9] Ignatius Donnelly to his wife, Donnelly Mss. October 26, 1865.

[10] These evaluations are quoted by Martin Ridge. Cf. Ridge, Martin. *Ignatius Donnelly: Portrait of a Politician*. St. Paul, Minnesota: Minnesota Historical Society, P. 290.

[11] *St. Paul Representative*, August 2, 9, 1893.

[12] *Minneapolis Representative*, September 8, 1894.

[13] *Ibid.*, November 13, 1895.

[14] *Ibid.*, January 1899.

[15]Donnelly Papers, Diary, June 29, 1885.

[16]As quoted in Hacker and Kendrick, *The United States Since 1865*. New York: F. S. Crofts & Co., 1935, pp. 304-05.

Chapter 2. Theodore Roosevelt: Patrician Renegade

[1]Judgments in this paragraph are quoted by Edmund Morris, *The Rise of Theodore Roosevelt*. New York: Modern Library Paperback Edition, 1979, p. xv

[2]*Ibid.*

[3]H. G. Wells. *Autobiography*. New York: Macmillan, 1934, p.649.

[4]Theodore Roosevelt. *Theodore Roosevelt: An Autobiography*. New York: Macmillan, 1913, p.57.

[5]Carleton Putnam. *Theodore Roosevelt: The Formative Years 1858-1886*. Vol. 1. New York: Scribner's, 1958, p. 236.

[6]*New York Tribune*, June 1, 1882

[7]*New York World*, February 6, 1884.

[8]*New York World*, July 21, 1884.

[9]Theodore Roosevelt. *Works*, ed. Hermann Hagedorn. Vol. I. National Edition. New York: Scribners, 1926, p. 107.

[10]DeAlva S. Alexander. *A Political History of New York State*. Vol. 4. New York: Henry Holt and Company, 1909, p. 82.

[11]See David McCullough's, *Mornings on Horseback*. New York: Simon & Schuster, 2003, pp. 344-45.

[12]*New York Times*, April 8, 1897.

[13]Matthew Josephson. *The Robber Barons*. New York: Harcourt, Brace, and World, Inc., 1962, p. 313.

[14]Clipping found in Theodore Roosevelt's Biography from a lecture given by Prof. Albert Bushnell Hart at Harvard University. Also, see Isabelle K. Savell's, *Daughter of Vermont: A Biography of Emily Eaton Hepburn*. N. Y. 1952, p. 106.

[15]As quoted by David McCullough, *The Path Between the Seas*, pp. 366-67.

[16]*Encyclopedia Britannica*, Vol. 19, p. 537.

[17]For a detailed description of this incredible venture, see Candice Millard's, *River of Doubt*. New York: Doubleday, 2005.

Chapter 3. Eugene Victor Debs: Rebel With Cause

[1]Ray Ginger. *The Bending Cross*. Chicago: Haymarket Books, 2007, p. 5.

[2]*Op. cit.*, p. 27.

³"Regardin' Terry Hut." *The Complete Works of James Whitcomb Riley.* Edited by Edmund Henry Eiteal. Vol. 3. Indianapolis: Bobbs-Merrill Company,1913, p. 326.

⁴David Karsner. *Debs: His Authorized Life and Letters.* New York: Boni and Liveright, 1919., p. 123.

⁵Numerous histories give reports on this strike. An excellent account can be found in Samuel Yellen.. *American Labor Struggles.* New York: Harcourt Brace and Company, 1969.

⁶ Ginger, *op. cit.,* p. 50.

⁷ *Debs: His Life, Writings, and Speeches.* Girard, Kansas: The Appeal to Reason, 1908, p.11.

⁸ *Chicago Tribune,* July 8, 1894, p. 1.

⁹ *Chicago Evening Post,* July 7, 1894.

¹⁰*Washington Post,* July 7, 1894.

¹¹ *New York Call,* April 29, 1919; also, *Appeal to Reason,* May 17, 1919

¹²Joseph Nathan Kane with Janet Podell & Steven Anzovin. *Facts About the Presidents.* Seventh edition. New York: Dublin & Company, 2001, p. 267, p.278, p. 290, respectively.

¹³ Marguerite Young. *Harp Song for a Radical: The Life and Times of Eugene Victor Debs.* New York: Knopf & Company, 1999.

¹⁴ *New York Call,* April 29, 1919; also, *Appeal to Reason,* May 17, 1919.

¹⁵ John Dos Passos. *USA.* New York: Modern Library, Random House, 1930, p. 151.

Chapter 4. Robert M. LaFollette: Unyielding Reformer

¹ Nancy Unger. *Fighting Bob La Follette: The Righteous Reformer.* Chapel Hill, North Carolina: University of North Carolina Press, 2000, p. 10.

² State Historical Society of Wisconsin at Madison, WI, Microfilm: Current, *Civil War,* 241.

³ David P. Thelen. *Robert M. La Follette: And the Insurgent Spirit.* Madison: University of Wisconsin Press, 1976., p. 4.

⁴ Unger, *op. cit.,* p. 53.

⁵ David P. Thelen. *Early Life of Robert M. La Follette 1855-1884.* Chicago: Loyola University Press, 1966, pp. 52-61.

⁶ Unger, *op. cit.,* pp. 78-79.

⁷ Thelen, *op. cit.,* p. 9.

⁸ *Ibid.,* p. 13.

⁹ John A. Garraty. "La Follette: The Promise Unfulfilled," *American Heritage,* Vol. 13 (April 1962), p. 84.

[10] *Yearbook of the United States Department of Agriculture, 1901,* pp. 699, 709, and 754.

[11] Thelen, *op. cit.,* pp. 29-30.

[12] Unger, *op. cit.,* pp. 118-19.

[13] *Ibid.,* p. 121.

[14] Garraty, *op. cit.,* p. 84.

[15] John D. Buenker, *The Progressive Era, 1893-1914.* Vol. 4. Madison, Wisconsin: State Historical Society, 1998, p. 467.

[16] Thelen, *op. cit.,* p. 54.

[17] Hacker and Kendrick, *op. cit..,* pp. 390-91.

[18] Elizabeth Frost, ed. *The Bully Pulpit.* New York: New England Associated, 1988, p. 183.

[19] Thelen, *op. cit.,* pp. 69-70.

[20] George E. Mowry. *The Era of Theodore Roosevelt and the Birth of Modern America 1900-1912.* New York: Harper and Row, 1958, p. 247.

[21] Herbert Quick, "Governor Bob," *Saturday Evening Post,* September 23, 1911.

[22] *Milwaukee Journal,* ca February, 1912.

[23] Joseph Nathan Kane. *Facts About the Presidents.* New York: Permabooks, 1959, p.300.

[24] As quoted by Thelen, *op. cit.,* p. 134.

[25] As quoted by Dayton David McKean, "Woodrow Wilson," *Hiistory and Criticism of American Public Address,* William Norwood Brigance, (ed.). Vol. 2. New York: Russell & Russell, p. 988.

[26] *Literary Digest,* Vol. 55. October 6, 1917, p. 15.

[27] "The War in Retrospect," *La Follette's Magazine,* Vol. 15., No. 24., April, 1920, pp. 70-71.

[28] *Encyclopedia of American Facts and Dates.* Sixth edition. New York: Thomas Y. Crowell Company., p. 454.

[29] Belle Case La Follette. "A Question of Democracy," *La Follette's Magazine,* No. 5. May 10, 1913.

[30] "Comments." Robert M. La Follette Papers, 1912.

[31] *Congressional Record,* Vol. 61 , pt. 6:6435.

Chapter 5. George W. Norris: Liberal Independent

[1] George W. Norris. *The Autobiography of George W. Norris.* New York: Macmillan, 1945, pp. 59-60.

[2] Paul W. Glad. *The Trumpet Soundeth. William Jennings Bryan and His Democracy, 1896-1912.* Lincoln, Nebraska: University of Nebraska Press, 1960, p. 48.

[3]Norris, *op. cit.*, pp.97-98.

[4]Francis Russell. *The Shadow of Blooming Grove: Warren G. Harding and His Times*. New York: McGraw-Hill Book Company, 1968, p. 232.

[5]As quoted by Unger, *op. cit.*, p. 249. Also, see *U. S. Congressional Record*, 65th Cong., 1st Sess. (April 4, 1917), Vol. 55, pt. 1, p. 215.

[6]Norris, *op. cit.*, 203.

[7]Longworth was married to Alice, daughter of Theodore Roosevelt. An anecdote which made the rounds during the time Longworth was Speaker recanted the morning he came into the House chambers and strode down the aisles before coming to a small group where a Democrat was speaking to fellow members. Longworth interrupted enough to pass his hand over the bald pate of the Democrat and remarked, "Tom, your head feels to me as smooth as my wife's bottom." Longworth basked in the titter evoked by his witticism until the victimized member, rubbed his own hand over his bald head, and rejoined, "By George! He's right!"

[8]*New York Times*, December 29, 1930, 1:4.

[9] Norris, *op. cit.*, 317.

[10] Ray Tucker, "Norris Surveys the Political Scene," *New York Times Magazine*, July 14, 1935, p. 3.

[11]As quoted by Joseph Lash, *Eleanor and Franklin*. New York: W. W. Norton & Co., 1971, p. 522.

[12]Richard Lowitt, *George W. Norris: The Triumph of a Progressive., 1933-1934*. New York: W. W. Norton & Sons, 1971, pp. 24-25. See also Harold Ickes, *Secret Diary: First Thousand Days*. New York: Simon & Schuster, 1953, p. 119.

[13]Lowitt, *op. cit.*, p. 430.

[14]*Washington Star*, November 4, 1942.

[15]*Lincoln Star*, November 4, 1942, Also, *New York Times*, November 5, 1942.

Chapter 6. Henry Agard Wallace: New Deal Reformist

[1]John C. Culver and John Hyde. *American Dreamer: A Life of Henry A. Wallace*. New York: W. W. Norton & Co., 2000, p. 12.

[2]*Ibid.*, p. 13.

[3]Iowa State University, Parks Library, Special Collections File, "Recollections of Henry A. Wallace at Iowa State."

[4]Culver and Hyde, *op. cit.*, p. 83. Ilo Wallace was amply rewarded; at the time of her death in 1981 at the age of ninety-three, Pioneer Hi-Bred recorded sales of $478 million and earned a net profit of $63.5 million. One-quarter of Pioneer's shares were held by Ilo and her children at the time. [5]"The Reminiscences of Henry Agard Wallace," Columbia University Oral History, p. 177.

[6]*Ibid.*, pp. 190-91.

[7]*Memoirs of Cordell Hull*, Vol. I, pp. 353-57. New York: Macmillan Co., 1948.

[8]Morison, Samuel Eliot. *The Oxford History of the American People*. New York: Oxford University Press, 1965, pp. 957-58.

[9]*Ibid.*, p. 965.

[10]As quoted, H. W. Brands. *The Privileged Life and Radical Presidency of Franklin Delano Roosevelt*. New York: Anchor Books, 2008. P. 429. Also, see U. S. Supreme Court Documents: Schechter Poultry Corp. vs. United States, Vol. 295, p. 405. See, too, Nathan Miller. *FDR: An Intimate History*. New York: Doubleday & Co., 1983, pp. 370-73, *passim.*

[11]William L. Langer and S. Everett Gleason. *The Challenge to Isolation 1937-1940*. Harper & Brothers, 1952, Pp. 82-85. Also, see Kenneth S. Davis. *FDR: Into the Storm 1937-1940*. New York: Random House, 1993, p. 437.

[12]Henry A. Wallace, "Farmer, Consumers and Middlemen and Their Food Supplies in Time of War," September 8, 1939, University of Iowa Library.

[13]*New York Times*, October 26, 1939.

[14]For a more detailed explanation of these "Guru" letters, see Culver and Hyde, *op. cit.*, pp. 132-46.

[15]Ted Morgan. *FDR: A Biography*. New York: Simon and Schuster. 1985, pp. 533-34.

[16]Donald Nelson. *Arsenal of Democracy: The Story of American War Production*. New York: Harcourt, Brace, 1946, p. 160.

[17]Herbert Eaton. *Presidential Timber: A History of Nominating Conventions 1868-1960*. London: The Free Press of Glencoe, Collier-Macmillan, 1964. P. 405.

[18]Quoted from an interview with Clark Clifford reprinted in Patrick Anderson, *The President's Men*. New York: Doubleday, 1968, p. 116. Also, see Rosenman, Oral History Transcript, p. 213, Harry S. Truman Library.

[19]*Public Papers of Harry S. Truman, 1946*, p. 216.

[20]Margaret Truman. *Harry S. Truman*. New York:William Morrow & Company, 1978, p. 309. [21]The letter from Mr. Wallace was written to the author in connection with research into speeches which had significant effects during the early Cold War period.

[22]Henry A. Wallace Papers, "Announcement Address," December 29, 1947, University of Iowa Library.

[23]This book's author was a graduate student writing about public persuasions at the time and was among attendees at the meeting held in the Chicago Arena.

Bibliography and Related Readings

Alexander, DeAlva S. *A Political History of New York State*. Vol. 4. New York: Henry Holt and Company, 1909.

Allen, Frederick Lewis. *The Great Pierpont Morgan*. New York: Harper & Row, 1949.

Beard, Charles A. and Mary Beard. *The Rise of American Civilization*. New York: Macmillan Company, 1927.

Bowers, Claude. *The Tragic Era*. New York: Houghton Mifflin Co., 1929.

Debs, Eugene V. *Debs: His Life, Writings, and Speeches*. Girard, Kansas: The Appeal to Reason, 1908.

Ginger. Ray. *The Bending Cross: A Biography of Eugene Victor Debs*. Chicago: Haymarket Books. 2007.

Hacker, Louis M. and Benjamin B. Kendrick. *The United States Since 1865*. New York: F. S. Crofts & Co., 1935.

Hagedorn, Hermann, (ed.). *Works: Theodore Roosevelt*. Vol. I. National Edition. New York: Scribner's, 1926.

Holbrook, Stewart H. *Lost Men of American History*. New York: Macmillan, 1946.

Jones, Eliot. *The Trust Problem in the United States*. New York: Macmillan Co., 1921.

Josephson, Matthew. *The Robber Barons — 1861-1901*. New York: Harcourt, Brace, and World, 1962.

Moody, John. *The Railroad Builders*. Princeton, N.J.: Yale University Press, 1919.

Morris, Edmund. *The Rise of Theodore Roosevelt*. New York: Random House, 1079.

Nevins, Allan. *Abram S. Hewitt: With Some Account of Peter Cooper*. New York: Harper & Brothers, 1935.

Pringle, H. F. *Theodore Roosevelt*. New York: Harcourt, Brace, and Co., 1931.

Safire, William. *Lend Me Your Ears: Great Speeches in History*. New York: W. W. Norton & Company, 1992.

Steffens, Lincoln. *The Autobiography of Lincoln Steffens*. Santa Clara, California: Heydey Books, 1981.

Stone, Irving. *Adversary in the House*. New York: Double Day & Co., Inc., 1947.

Tarbell, Ida. *History of the Standard Oil Company*. New York: Macmillan Co., 1904.

Unger, Nancy C. *Fighting Bob La Follette: Righteous Reformer*. Chapel Hill, N.C.: University of North Carolina Press, 2000.

Veblen, Thorstein. *Theory of the Leisure Class*. New York: Viking Press, 1924.

Yellen, Samuel. *American Labor Struggles*. New York: Harcourt Brace & Co., 1969.

Photographs

Ignatius Donnelly, p. 7. From a reprint in Ridge, Martin. *Ignatius Donnelly: Portrait of a Politician.* St. Paul, MN: Minnesota Historical Society Press, 1991,

Theodore Roosevelt. p. 23. From a reprint in Morris, Edmund. *The Rise of Theodore Roosevelt.* New York: Random House, 1979.

Robert LaFollette. p. 45. From a reprint in Unger, Nancy. *Fighting Bob LaFollette: The Righteous Reformer.* Chapel Hill, NC: University of North Carolina Press, 2000.

Eugene Debs. p. 65. From a reprint in Ginger, Ray. *The Bending Cross: A Biography of Eugene V. Debs.* Chicago, Ill: Haymarket Press, 2007.

George Norris. p. 95. From a reprint in *Fighting Liberal: The Autobiography of George W. Norris.* 2nd. ed. Lincoln, Nebraska: University of Nebraska Press, 1992.

Henry Wallace. p. 117. From a reprint in Culver, John C. and John Hyde. *American Dreamer: A Life of Henry A. Wallace.* New York: W. W. Norton & Company, 2000.

Index

A

Addams, Jane, 92, 100
Adams, John, 3
Aldrich, Nelson, 78
Altgeld, John P., 18
American Federation of Labor, 50, 51
American Railway Union (ARU)
    formation of, 52
    membership, 52
American Sugar Refining Company, 35, 38
Anthony, Susan B., 47, 89, 90
Antietam, 3
Atheneum Company, 9
Armour, Phil D., 14
Aylesworth, Burton A., 17

B

Bacon, Francis, 10
Bacon, Robert, 25
Ballinger, Richard, 98
Barkely, Alben, 134
Berger, Victor, 58
Bettrich, Marguerite Marie, 46, 63
Beveridge, Albert, 80
Bimetallism, 14
Blaine, James G., 29
Boas, Franz, 92
Borah, William, 80
Bourbon Democrats, 20

Bourne, Jonathan, 80
Bowles, Chester, 135
Breckinridge, John C., 14
Bristow, Joseph, 80
Brodhead, May, 118
Brown, Norris, 80
Bryan, William Jennings, 21, 38, 84, 86, 101, 102, 149, 152
Burkett, Elmer, 80
Burton's Anatomy of Melancholy, 10
Bryant, George E., 69
Byrnes, James, 114, 134, 136, 137

C

Cannon, Joseph G., 98
Carow, Edith, 33, 44
Carver, George Washington, 119
Case, Belle, 68, 89, 152
Cassady, Simon, 122
Chancellorsville, 3
Chafin, Eugene Wilder, 82
Chapman, Oscar, 135
Chicago Tribune, 55, 151
Churchill, Winston, 1, 136, 138, 140
Cincinnati Press, 84
Civil Service System, 28
Clapp, Moses, 80, 84
Cleveland, Grover, 12, 17, 19, 28, 30, 50, 56, 122
Cleveland, Ohio, 59, 92, 96
Clifford, Clark, 135, 154
Coolidge, Calvin, 93, 105